CW00969063

THE AUTOBIOGRAPHY

From a rickety old caravan in '60's Ireland, via Germany and bonny Scotland, to the leafy suburbs of southern England, a Forces Brat battles his way to manhood, ably hindered by his large and eccentric family.

A true coming-of-age tale that will have you laughing until your bum falls off.

Contains attitudes of the times, which the author finds offensive.

Acclaim for *The Autobiography*:

"A literary masterpiece."
Mum

"I couldn't put it down."
Superglue Magazine

"A cracking good read, but not enough mention of rats and mice."
Small Rodents Weekly

"The story rattles along at a great pace."
Gilbert the Snail

THE AUTOBIOGRAPHY

ANONYMOUS

Anonymous   Chesterfield

1. Edition, 2024

Copyright © J.R. Mulholland 2024

Gilbert House

Sterland Street

Chesterfield S40 1BP

Anonymous asserts the moral right to be identified as the author of this work.

For my

Big brother,

Jock

PREFACE

This work is going to differ from most autobiographies in that they are usually written by famous people. I intend to become famous by writing my autobiography.

The other main difference is that I don't intend to sign it. I have always wanted to be famous without the drawback of anyone knowing who I am. You may laugh, but it has been done before. Jack the Ripper, Banksy, Ed Davey, and the stray dog that bonked the Queen's corgi, are but a few examples that spring to mind. They all had their own techniques and I have mine. They have nothing to fear from me – especially not the corgi.

The difficulty is knowing where to begin. Perhaps, with an autobiography, this shouldn't be a problem, but it is. Should I start with my earliest memories, my first significant experiences, or at a point where the public might be vaguely interested, such as when I became famous?

The last idea appeals to me but, as this book is my sole claim to fame, I'd have had to wait for it to be published before I could start writing.

I've therefore decided to start at the beginning.

CHAPTER 1

THE GATHERING STORM

Nine months before I was born, I went to a party with my dad and came home with my mum. I do not remember being conceived of course, but I was once taken back by a hypnotherapist and my earliest memory was of floating contentedly, surrounded in warm, comforting water, listening to the sound of my mother's heartbeat. The hypnotherapist's excitement was shattered when I announced we were in the local swimming pool.

My happy days in the womb were rudely interrupted roughly nine months after that fateful Christmas party, and I found myself being pushed, shoved and generally forced in a direction in which I had no intention of going. I held on tenaciously for two weeks but eventually my strength gave out. As my mother gave one final push I came out swinging, two weeks overdue.

"It's a boy," cried the midwife when she saw me swinging.

"He'll be a boxer when he grows up," laughed the nurse. Apparently I was swinging punches in every direction.

I started yelling my head off as soon as the midwife

picked me up, and so avoided the slap on the bottom which I had been so dreading - the slap that sent so many youngsters out into the world with a sore bum, a chip on their shoulder, and a strong desire to get even.

Being so young I was not sure if I had escaped the slap because I was yelling or because I had been swinging punches. This, combined with the fact that yelling louder than any other baby in the ward invariably led to me being the first to be fed, had a profound influence on the first twelve years of my life, which I spent yelling and punching. Occasionally I laughed as well – usually after punching someone.

I also spent a considerable amount of time eating. I would eat anything as long as it was totally indigestible. Starting off with coal then working my way through batteries and big-brand baby food, I eventually set about the ambitious task of eating my pram. Half the stuffing and enough of the nuts and bolts to make things decidedly unstable (both the pram and my guts), disappeared down my greedy gullet before I was discovered and dragged off to the doctor. I was the only baby around who had to have his nappy changed on a regular basis to avoid rusting.

"What has he eaten today?" chuckled our little Indian doctor who seemed to enjoy my regular visits.

He went on chuckling, I went on eating, and my parents went on patiently waiting to see what missing household items might turn up in my nappies. It once took them a week to finish a game of tiddlywinks.

My brother had already got two years life experience under his belt when I was born. He was called Jock, which was a strange name to give an Irish lad, but Dad insisted it would come in handy if we ever moved to Scotland.

When my parents first brought me home from the hospital, Jock, who had been warned to be on his best behaviour when the new baby came home, gave me his favourite toy car to play with.

"What a daft thing to give a baby," I thought and promptly chucked it out of my cot. He was not overly impressed at this rejection of his peace-offering, and regarded me with mild resentment from then on. I could not understand this resentment until a year later when my brother Harold was born.

Harold made his appearance when I was barely one year old, thus depriving me of the attention that I rightfully deserved. Mum and Dad called me over to his cot to introduce me to him.

"Yuchhh!!!" I said.

He hadn't even got the common decency to reply to my heart-felt greeting.

Dad told me that babies are delicate, and that I was not to punch him until he was older.

I could hardly wait!

I was always jealous of Harold, for no reason in particular. Harold, of course, made the most of my jealousy and baited me at every available opportunity with irritating squeaks and gurgles that seemed to delight our parents, but that bugged the life out of me. Even his annoying crying got him picked up, cuddled and fed. He soon caught on to this old ploy and cried night and day. I decided to give it a go myself, but whenever I tried I was told to shut up or I'd be given something to cry about.

Talk about double standards. When he pretended to cry he got a mouthful of Mother's mammaries. If I tried it I got a gobful from Dad.

I hated that child. I was aching to thump him, but I remembered Dad's warning. I bided my time until he was old enough, then I laid into him.

It was great.

While I was eagerly looking forward to my next excuse to batter him, Harold had not been idle. He had been busy planning a defence in depth that was to take me ages to fathom out and adopt effective counter-measures to.

Ready to put his system to the test, Harold made a sneak-and-run attack on me. Delighted that he had struck first, thus reducing the severity of Dad's punishment for my part in the forthcoming carnage, I raced eagerly after him. I was close on his heels and about to pounce when he leapt up, twisting in mid-air, and landed on his back on Dad's high-backed, high-sided armchair, with his legs pointing out at me like twin cannon. I fell on him like the French cavalry at Agincourt, and was promptly propelled backwards across the room to make a painful landing via the far wall.

Incensed at this unexpected setback, I picked myself up and threw myself back into the fray. Several more furious but futile frontal attacks were launched and repulsed before Dad intervened and put an end to the proceedings, uttering those now immortal words, "C'est magnifique, mais n'est pas la guerre."

I brooded for a couple of days then came up with the

4

idea of outflanking the legs. It would not be easy because of the height of the sides of the chair – but if I was quick...?

I struck. The legs came up. I feinted to the right, darted to the left then sprung like a rampaging tortoise. I was halfway over the armrest when ...THUNNKK!!! ...the twin barrels of his heavy artillery swung round in the nick of time and shot me across the room. I bounded back, put in a diversionary frontal attack then side-stepped and went for the right flank. ...THWACKK!!! ...I was down again - but I had nearly made it.

Encouraged by this I made several more attempts on his embedded position over the following weeks but, although the speed, cunning and agility of my attacks improved on a daily basis, he was improving the pace of his defensive twists and turns at a disproportionate rate, and his thigh muscles were becoming alarmingly powerful with the daily exercise of propelling me across the room. He was also aided by the fact that the seat of the armchair had become worn smooth by his rapidly rotating buttocks, and he could now spin on it like a top.

Then, at last, he made his first mistake. Having perfected his defensive technique on me, he now felt ready to take on the muscular might of big brother Jock. Following some minor slight on his character, Harold made one of his trade-mark hit-and-run attacks then entrenched himself in the armchair behind the fearsome twin mortars of his legs. Full of the confidence that his extra size and years gave him, Jock moved in for the kill. Admittedly he did not fly as far across the room as I normally did, but he hit the floor just as hard.

5

Humiliated, he tore back in for a frenzied full-frontal attack and I have to admit to feeling a grudging admiration for the way Harold tenaciously held him off. But with those extra years came extra cunning and experience and a knowledge of the strategic, tactical and logistical advantages of alliances. Jock persuaded me to join in the attack. Callously sacrificing me on a suicidal frontal assault on the main position, Jock swept in from the exposed flank, got in behind the heavy guns, and gave young Harold the beating of his short life. By the time I had picked myself up off the floor and flung myself into the slaughter, it was all over. Dad had appeared and put a stop to the battle. I'd missed my chance. However, I was happy in the knowledge of the secret of bridging Harold's defences, and assumed that my chance would come. Unfortunately for me, Harold proved more adept at forging alliances than I did and so, over the next few years, I had to content myself with a few minor successes from surprise attacks in armchairless locations.

At that time, we had a lovely dog called 'Paddy', which was also Dad's nickname in the RAF. He was a Golden Retriever (the dog, not Dad) but was the size of an Irish Wolfhound. He was enormous. He was also very intelligent, had a wonderful temperament, loved children, but had a pathological hatred of cats and dustbin men.

His best friend was a big, gangly Afghan Hound whose name we never knew as dogs can't talk. He actually used to knock on the door and wait for Paddy to be let out to play. They would bound away together, hurdling the neighbours' fences. That was their favourite game. One neighbour did try to complain once, but my mother threw such a fit when she told her that Paddy had been streaking across her garden with an Afghan, that no one ever tried again. My poor father got an earful when he arrived home, and it took him some time to convince Mum that he'd been at work all day and had been nowhere near the neighbours' gardens.

Paddy was a dog of many faces, all of them hairy. On the one paw he was very sensitive and hated hearing the children being scolded and so, to prevent this, he would not allow us to do anything naughty. For example, when Jock was younger, if he crawled too close to the fire, Paddy would grab him by the nappy and drag him away. Now that may not seem to you to be a particularly brave or heroic thing to do, but that is because you do not yet know about Jock's early bowel movements. He suffered (everybody suffered) from an odd complaint sometimes found in small babies where, instead of the usual gentle, infantile squirt of semi-liquid doo-doos, he formed rock-hard little turds which he would shoot across the room like armour-piercing bullets. (There is a medical term for it – but I'm beginning to doubt if the words my father used had anything to do with medicine.) This was not normally a problem once Jock's nappy was firmly held in place by means of an extra-large, reinforced safety pin. The dangerous time was when his nappy was being changed. Nappy-changing time was a danger to the world at large if my mother was careless where she was pointing him, and a danger to Jock himself if Dad was changing him as he would invariably plunge the unwieldy great safety pin through the poor little mite's foreskin as well as the nappy, then spend the next thirty minutes trying to work out why he was still screaming after he'd been fed and changed.

The main danger was, of course, to Paddy who was always in danger of losing a tooth whilst in action. Visitors, watching in fascination as Paddy took a firm hold on Jock's nappy and dragged him away from the fire, never did find out why he would occasionally fly backwards across the room then scamper away howling.

Paddy's downsides were his blind hatred of cats, and a love of fighting. Mum hated taking him for walks because Paddy would be dragging her one way, trying to get at other dogs, and I'd be dragging her the other way, trying to get at other kids.

His main enemy was a big Boxer called Sabre. Sabre was the bully of the patch and was top dog in the area. When a young Paddy had appeared on the scene, despite the fact he was still only a puppy, Sabre attacked him. He didn't really hurt him and was just letting him know who was boss, but Paddy never forgave him. The very next day he set about training and eating to make himself big and strong enough for the eventual showdown. He ate like a horse and used to gallop along beside our car when we drove into town. We'd arrive first, but it was never long before Paddy would come loping around the corner, tongue lolling out, and stand there panting beside us. While we were shopping, Paddy would make his own rounds. A couple of local butchers had taken a shine to him, and he would go from one to the other collecting his free sausages, bones and various, nutritious left-overs. The one dietary indulgence he allowed himself was lollipops, which Jock used to share with him lick for lick.

He indirectly involved my father in his training program one day. He was out on a fitness run around the local lake when he upended Dad's commanding officer, who was out fishing, and landed him in the water. Paddy made his getaway before his dog tags could be examined but the CO recognised his rapidly retreating rear-end, and had a quiet word with Dad about controlling his dog.

As well as working on his size, strength and stamina, Paddy did not neglect his sparring practice and emerged victorious from many minor skirmishes with the lesser dogs of the patch. He finally decided he was ready for Sabre after a rather unfortunate incident involving a friend of his, a big Alsatian called Fritz. Fritz had been sleeping in our back garden after playing with Paddy when Dad arrived home from work and tripped over him. Startled, the dog went for him. Paddy piled in like a freight train, bowling the other dog over, and savaging it. It took off down the road at a great rate of knots and refused to play with Paddy again. Fritz didn't realise how lucky he had been. If Paddy hadn't appeared when he did, then my father would have turned on him. Not a pretty prospect I can assure you.

Once when Dad was between jobs and delivering groceries from Grampa's shop on the Lisburn Road, Belfast, an old lady opened her door and her Labrador ran out, bit him, then ran back into what it mistakenly believed was the safety of its own house. Never one to turn the other cheek, Dad charged in after it, elbowing the old lady out of the way. He cornered it in the kitchen and gave the terrified animal a good slap. As he left, the dog came to the door, keeping well behind its owner and giving its drooping tail a few tentative wags in the hope that he wouldn't go for it again.

"Oh look," gasped the old woman as she struggled up from the floor where she'd been sent sprawling. "He's forgiven you."

Dad looked down at the blood seeping through his torn trouser leg but decided to say nothing as she was worth a large sack of King Edwards, a cucumber and a couple of cabbages a week to Granddad's business.

At a later date, Jock was having trouble with a nasty dog on his paper round. The owner must have known what his dog was like, but he still regularly let it out in the mornings where it would chase my brother every time he delivered the paper. Jock was scared, so Dad decided to accompany him on his next delivery to see if he could make the dog and its owner see reason.

Early next morning they arrived at the house. The garden gate creaked open then banged loudly shut as Dad made sure the dog would hear them. True to form the old mongrel came charging around the corner of the house but, instead of finding Jock racing for the gate, it found our father waiting for it.

Taking one look at his vengeful visage it turned and tried to run, but it was too late. Dad had it by the collar. He hoisted it off the ground and pinned it up against the side of the porch. As its tongue lolled out and its legs kicked frantically, the door opened and its equally cantankerous old owner appeared, staring in disbelief at the sight in front of him.

"Just making friends with your dog," Dad said cheerily as he lowered it to the ground and gave it a couple of friendly, but firm, pats as it lay there gasping for breath. The owner spluttered and growled and threatened, but from then on the dog was always locked inside when Jock delivered the paper.

But I digress. Paddy finally decided he was ready to take on Sabre and went looking for him. Sabre was not a difficult dog to find and Paddy had no difficulty in finding him. The Boxer had been itching for this encounter and, when he saw Paddy coming, he spat out the Poodle he'd been playing with, and turned to face him.

Old Sabre was a big, nasty, experienced street-fighter but, like many bullies, he began to panic when things weren't going his way. Paddy's long, loping training runs to the local butchers had paid off, and he was now bigger, stronger and fitter than the older dog. Sabre fought viciously, but Paddy gradually got on top as the fight went on and the older dog began to tire. He tried to give in, rolling over, but Paddy would not let up and, by the time my father arrived and pulled him off, Sabre was in a bit of a state, and had to be taken to the vet, with Dad footing the bill. Sabre lived to fight another day, but left Paddy well alone after that.

Paddy was now top-dog in neighbourhood and strutted around his territory challenging any dog that he didn't know. Dad thought this was fantastic, but Mum hated it.

She said she would prefer a lapdog to a fighting one. Paddy, as sensitive as ever, sat on her lap. She quickly came round to Dad's way of thinking.

Paddy's other character flaw was his blind hatred of cats. This is inherent in most dogs, but with Paddy it was an obsession. He had been scratched as an inquisitive puppy, spent the next year terrified of cats and then, on discovering that they were more scared of him, spent the rest of his life chasing them at any chance. He once wrecked a neighbour's house when he chased a cat in through an open door, up the stairs, round the bedrooms and back out again.

An intelligent dog, Paddy knew his highway code. He would stop at the kerb before crossing a road, look right and left, and up and down as well just to be sure. His hatred of cats though, proved to be his undoing. He was taking a stroll down the lane with my father, who never had him on a lead, when he spotted a cat across the road. He darted straight out and was knocked down by a passing car. He died in the arms of my dad, who was distraught.

Again there was a bit of a misunderstanding. Before Mum had heard the news, a neighbour took her in, sat her down and gave her a glass of brandy. Fearing the worst, Mum said, "It's Paddy, isn't it?" The neighbour confirmed that it was. Mum was in bits, and her friend tried to console her by saying that Paddy had been a lovely dog. To the neighbour's astonishment, Mum started laughing hysterically. She'd thought that Dad had been killed.

Friends knew how upset my parents were and encouraged them to go straight out and buy another dog to replace Paddy. This they did, and ended up with a fully-grown little ragamuffin of a terrier, who had been spoilt rotten for years by his elderly owner, called Bongo (the dog, not the owner).

It was a mistake from the start. Poor, little Bongo could never take Paddy's place in my parents' hearts. He had been used to being the centre of attention when he was the only love in the life of his previous, now deceased, owner. Having to share my parents with three young children was not something that pleased him, and he would do anything to get their attention.

His favourite game was swinging on the washing on the clothes line and seeing what he could pull down. I used to join in too, and blame Bongo for the consequences. He would become jealous when Mum was bathing the children, and he'd jump in with us.

Dad tried to teach him a few tricks but, unlike Paddy who enjoyed it and was keen to learn, Bongo was having none of that nonsense. He tried to teach him to sit up and beg and, to be fair to him, Bongo did try, but he had splayed feet and, whenever he sat up on his hind legs he would promptly roll over backwards.

Unable to train him in even the basic niceties of life, Mum found him a real handful as she was trying to bring up three young children at the same time and, whereas Paddy had been a help, Bongo was a considerable hindrance. As Dad was being posted abroad, they gave Bongo to a lonely old neighbour of ours who doted on him. We saw him shortly afterwards, our scruffy little Bongo, strutting down the street, groomed and gleaming,

13

thoroughly spoilt again, and answering to the name of 'Barnaby'. He stuck his nose in the air and turned his head away as he passed us by. He'd moved up in the world.

That was the last we saw of Bongo.

CHAPTER 2

INTO BATTLE

My father was posted abroad when I was one year old, with Harold aged only a few months and with his years as an armchair hero still some time in front of him. Dad abandoned us in Belfast and set off on his travels. Jock was three, so Dad left him in charge

We eventually made it over to Germany. Fortunately for us, that was where Dad was stationed. The town was called, 'Jever' but Harold pronounced it, 'Mama' because it was the only word he could say. I was fourteen months older and could say lots of words, but none of the locals seemed to understand me. It was extremely frustrating'

"Where can a boy get an ice-cream around here, me old cock?" I would ask politely.

"Was für ein feiner großer Junge," they would say – and they were right, but that didn't help me get my choppers around a large dollop of ice-cream.

I bent the whole of my tiny intellect to solving this problem and was eventually to come up with a rather drastic but exceedingly successful solution. But meanwhile there was a knock at the door.

"Guten Morgen," called a gruff voice outside.

Curious, I opened the door an inch.

"Guten Morgen," he said again. My ears had not deceived me.

I decided to join in this strange game. "Murten Gorgon," I replied.

"Ich heisse, Herr Harms," he informed me.

I looked at his one good arm then at the other which finished just below the elbow with a large metal hook attached where, in my meagre experience, most people had hands.

"I've got two harms," I told him, holding them up as proof. He took one of them in his good hand.

"Wo ist dein Mama, Junge?" he spat in that harsh, guttural snarl that German's use when talking to children, sweet-hearts, bank managers, criminals and anyone else no matter what the subject.

'Junge!' I recognised that word. It was the word people used when I asked them for ice-cream. There had to be a connection there somewhere.

"Maaammmy," I yelled, freeing myself from his good hand and swinging on his hook in my excitement. "Maaammmyyyy, the ice-queam man's here."

"Come down off there," shouted my horrified mother as she appeared from the kitchen. "Let go of *that*!"

I'm not sure if she was horrified because she was afraid that I would embarrass Herr Harms by swinging on his hook, or because she was scared of it and didn't want me anywhere near it. She has always sworn the former, but I suspect the latter.

"Get down NOW," she yelled at me then, more quietly to Herr Harms, "I'm terribly sorry. He gets up to all sorts."

Herr Harms though, was pleased as Punch that I'd taken a shine to his hook. He smiled and patted me on the head with his good hand. The local children were terrified of it. They made the mistake of swinging on his good hand and so ended up being patted on the head with the hook.

I loved that hook. Jock and I used to fight over who would hold the hook if Herr Harms, who was our neighbour, took us for a walk. I thought that everyone should have one – especially my dad. I begged, pleaded and cajoled him, but he steadfastly refused to chop his hand off. So much for his claim that he would do anything for his kids.

Faced with Dad's obstinacy, I decided to take matters into my own hands. I slipped Jock's Swiss Army Knife under my pillow that night, saw-blade extended and ready, and I waited for Dad to go to bed. At last his eyes closed and he drifted off into a deep sleep. My chance had come. Unfortunately by this time I had been asleep for a good two hours and the plan had to be shelved.

But I digress. Herr Harms was still standing in our doorway with me swinging on his hook and Mum trying to discreetly prize me off it. He produced some flowers.

"Gift fur das Kinder," he stated, emphasising the word 'gift'.

"Oh, thank you," said Mum, taking them from him and handing them to Jock and me.

"NEIN, NEIN, NEIN," shouted the old man, snatching

17

them back again. "GIFT. GIFT. GIFT!"

He backed out thinking the British were all mad and leaving us thinking that the Germans were a bit mean with their presents.

When Dad arrived home, Mum told him the story. For weeks he had been practising his schoolboy German by talking very slowly and loudly at the locals – mainly in English. However, he recognised the word 'gift', as meaning 'poison'.

"Oh, that nice, old man," cried Mum. "He was trying to tell me it was poison. I must go and thank him."

I was shocked and couldn't understand why she wanted to thank him for trying to give poison to her children. It wasn't until I had kids of my own, that I understood.

Herr Harms had lost his hand in the First World War and lost his only son in the Second World War which had only finished fifteen years earlier but, even though we were British and my father was in the RAF, he was always very kind to us.

I was now absorbed by the problem of how to procure sufficient quantities of ice-cream for a boy of my gargantuan appetite but extremely limited grasp of the German language.

"Hoobeensea oy ice-cream?" I'd venture.

"Haben Sie ein was?" they'd ask.

"HOOBY DOOBY D'ICE-CREAM," I'd yell at the top of my voice, trying my father's tried and tested (and totally useless) method of communicating with foreigners.

It didn't work.

"Was für ein feiner großer Junge," they'd say and pat me on the head.

I fetched big brother Jock, and he tried out his more sophisticated German.

"Ent school dee bum-biter," he asked.

He had their attention. Things were looking up.

"Wo heir kann boy ein ice-cream be-gobbling?" he tried hopefully.

It failed.

"WO HEIR KANN BOY EIN ICE-CREAM BE-GOBBLING?" he explained slowly at the top of his voice. Dad had taught us well.

"Du sprichst Kauderwelsch, Junge," he was told.

We gave up in despair. "Dangle Shaun," I said anyway. Mum always maintained that politeness hurts no one.

"Was für ein feiner großer Junge," someone said as we left. It seemed to be some sort of conspiracy.

Jock sent me out to try again. "Break a leg," he shouted after me in encouragement. The scales fell away from my eyes. That was it! The answer! Jock was playing with his toy building blocks in the front room, I burst in, tripped over them, landed awkwardly and broke my left femur. Perfect! My plan was underway.

Mum took me to see the doctor. "Was für ein feiner großer Junge," he said when he saw me.

'It must be working,' I thought. That's what they said when I mentioned ice-cream. The doctor must know about my plan.

"Der ist noting wrong mit diesem boy," he proclaimed.

"Yes there is," insisted my mother. "I think he's broken

19

his leg."

"Nonsense!" The doctor poo-pooed the idea. "If das Bien ... um ... leg ...vas broken, zen he vould be weinen ... crying – nicht grinning all over his ... face."

So he didn't know about the ice-cream plot after all. Or worse, he knew about it and intended to foil my plans.

My mother angrily snatched me up (which hurt). "You don't know John," she snapped as she carried me out.

She took me twenty miles to the RAF hospital where they took X-rays and discovered a spiral fracture running the length of my left thigh. They put my leg in plaster from crutch to toe. I was delighted. My plan had worked. Now all that remained was to sally forth and test public reaction.

Unfortunately in my excitement I wet myself. It ran down the inside of the plaster cast and left me with a maddening, unscratchable itch right down my leg. Taking pity on me, Mum bought me a long, wooden ruler that I would thrust down the inside of the plaster cast and scratch like crazy with a look of sheer bliss on my face. To this day I cannot keep an ecstatic look off my face whenever I have my ruler in my hand.

Apart from this minor setback, and the fact that I had to have my broken leg propped up on books whenever I used the potty, my plan was a complete success. As I struggled to walk any distance, I had to share Harold's pram whenever Mum took us into town. I made sure that the leg in plaster always protruded from the pram so that passers-by would notice.

"Was für ein feiner großer Junge," they would smile, and the ice-creams flew in from all directions.

"Dangle Shaun," I'd say.

"Mama," said Harold who, as my side-kick in the pram, also got his share.

"Bastard," said Jock who didn't get any free ice-cream and had to walk while we were paraded around in the luxury of the pram. He knew a conspiracy when he saw one. He knew it had all been planned.

Being a wee lass from the Shankill, Mum found it a bit intimidating mixing with the snooty RAF types she now found herself amongst. She tried hard to fit in and listened intently to anything Dad said about flying, so she would have something to talk about at formal dinners in the officers' mess. One evening my father came home complaining that 'Ginger' had been flying too close to him for comfort. "He was right up my chuff," he said. Thinking this was a technical term for a part of the aircraft, Mum stored this little snippet of information away for future use.

Her chance to shine came at an RAF dinner the following day. As the oh-so-polite chitchat moved around the table, carefully avoiding my mother's place, she finally picked up the courage to show off some of her new-found expertise. Taking advantage of a lull in the conversation, she cleared her throat and took the plunge.

"So, Ginger," she announced loudly in her Belfast accent. "I hear you were up Paddy's chuff last night."

A deafening silence greeted this unexpected announcement, then Ginger began stuttering, "Who? M-m-me? I n-never…"

It took Dad a long time to see the funny side. As for Ginger, his reputation never fully recovered. A broken man, he resigned his commission soon after.

Meanwhile, I was making friends with the local children. Mum had left me in a playpen in the front garden, and Jock was keeping me company. An older lad climbed in and started pushing him around.

'What a good game,' I thought whilst looking round for a weapon to allow me to participate effectively despite my diminutive stature. I spotted a big, metal, toy car that looked like it might do the trick. Raising it high in the air I brought it crashing down on the back of the boy's unsuspecting head. They don't make them like that anymore. It was hardly even dented.

'That's German engineering for you,' I thought as the bully hopped around the playpen holding his battered head.

"YEEEOOOOWWWWWW!!!" he yelled.

"YEEEOOOOWWWWWW!!!" I yelled back gleefully. German wasn't so difficult when you got the hang of it.

I wanted to play some more but our new-found friend climbed out of the playpen and ran off up the road howling like a banshee as I yelled and whooped behind him. He later confessed to my mum that he was scared of her baby.

I would like to warn any children reading this, not to try this at home. Nowadays, your plastic car would smash to pieces and your friendly local bully would fetch his mates and beat the shite out of you.

After the incident with the metal car, no other children

came to play with us for a while and Jock became lonely and homesick.

"Do you remember good old Belfast?" he sighed nostalgically.

"No!" I replied wistfully.

"Do you remember Paddy?"

I did have a vague recollection of a big, hairy face that used to stare at me over the side of my pram from between two massive paws. I was slightly confused though because my father's friends in the RAF called *him* Paddy. When Dad came home from work that evening and poked his head around the pushchair to look at me, I studied his face intently then concluded that he must have started shaving. I was pleased that he had stopped licking my face as well.

By now I was two years old, blond, blue-eyed - and the Germans loved me. I had it made and loved my time in Germany. Harold loved it too. The culture suited him well. It was there that he was introduced, at an early age, to his two greatest loves – singing and drinking.

One day Mum went out, taking Jock and me with her, but leaving young Harold with Frau Schau, the house-keeper. When we arrived back home a couple of hours later, there was no sign of either of them. Mum got into a panic and hurried round to Frau Schau's house. There was no one in, but we could hear loud, raucous singing coming from next door. Above the general cacophony a deep and booming, but unmistakably baby, baritone bellowed tunelessly but enthusiastically along to the German drinking songs.

We looked through the window. A party was in full swing and there at the table, in the midst of all these big, beer-swilling Germans, was Harold. He had a bun in one hand and a small beaker of beer in the other, and he was singing away at the top of his voice. When Mum dragged him off home he cried his eyes out – a scene that was to be repeated many times when he was older.

Harold was normally a well-behaved child, compared to Jock and me, and caused no trouble – except when he was partying hard with the locals. My misbehaviour came from my obsession with wilfully and joyfully breaking all the rules I could find. I loved rules and would try to learn as many as I could so that I would have more to break. In Jock's case it was his willingness to be helpful and act on his own initiative that got him into hot water.

For example, Mum was out gardening one day and, realising that Jock had disappeared indoors on his own (which was unusual for him), she went back inside and found him hosing down the living room with the garden hose.

"I'm just washing the walls for you, Mummy," he announced proudly.

Jock was a little upset because he didn't get the praise he was expecting. Mum did say a few things, but I couldn't understand the words. 'Must be German,' I decided.

Harold's only real vice was that he could not resist the lure of the jam cupboard. He always had his sticky little fingers in the jam pot. Although my parents were painfully aware of the lack of jam in the house and of the smug, syrupy expression on Harold's sticky face, they never actually caught him in the act. He was like lightening. In, gobble, out, wipe, hide. They knew it wasn't me because I'd have admitted it for the attention, and Jock was too well-behaved. It had to be Harold, but he was the Ninja jam gobbler and couldn't be caught.

While my brother was decimating the jam supplies, Dad had been caught perpetrating some equally serious crime with roughly the same threat to the security of the country and the discipline of Her Majesty's armed forces as Harold's jam eating. As punishment they grounded him and, instead of flying, he found himself as second-in-command of a punishment squadron that set up air-to-ground targets for the less-naughty pilots to practice on. This was at RAF Nordhorn on the German/Dutch border.

A lot of the men in the squadron were there for disciplinary reasons and in general they were a pretty bad-assed lot – so Dad got on well with them. He got off to a good start on his first night in the combined officers and NCO's mess. One of the NCO's, Nobby, had an 'amusing' way of welcoming new arrivals. He would buy them a pint of brown ale in a pewter tankard and surreptitiously drop his false teeth in so, when the poor, unsuspecting tippler reached the bottom of his pint, he would have a close and unpleasant encounter with Nobby's gnashers. Luckily some kind-hearted soul took pity on him and tipped Dad off as to Nobby's favourite little prank.

When the be-dentured beverage was duly proffered, Dad was ready. He thanked Nobby profusely then pretended to take a drink as the vultures all watched him from the corners of their eyes, waiting for him to reach the bottom. Pulling a face, he announced in a loud voice to all the expectant people around him that the beer was 'off' and that it was going straight down the toilet. With that he took off towards the latrines with a frantic, gummy-faced little man desperately trying to catch him up. Dad reached the toilets first, slipped the dentures into his pocket, poured the beer down the lavatory and flushed the chain. He left poor Nobby, mumbling murderously, with his arm halfway round the S-bend, and returned to the Mess where he produced the dentures to rapturous applause. After that he could do no wrong.

At this time our baby-sitters were all hand-picked by Dad, who used it as a form of punishment for the more unruly elements amongst the men. They would glass a local in a vicious pub brawl on a Friday night then end up baby-sitting for us on the Saturday. It was a punishment they all grew to fear. Discipline improved dramatically and Dad was promoted to Flight Lieutenant.

Always ready to take up a new hobby, Dad found a book on judo. He and a friend bought a couple of judo suits and started learning a few throws from the book. It was basically trial and error with the blind leading the blind. A few short weeks later the RAF held a fancy-dress ball at the station. Dad wore his judo suit, complete with a hastily purchased black belt for effect. As the drink flowed and the hours got smaller, Dad's tales grew taller. This was the early 1960s and judo was still fairly new in the West and had an aura of mystique about it. By the end of the evening everyone was left in no doubt that my father was a martial arts expert and not a man to be trifled with. This proved to have been an unwise seed to have sown. He was summoned to the presence of his Commanding Officer the following day.

"Ahem…. I hear that you're something of a judo expert, Flight Lieutenant?" he said off-handedly.

"Wellll…. not really, sir," Dad replied truthfully but in an equally nonchalant manner. He was quite enjoying his new-found fame.

Encouraged by my father's modesty, the CO went on. "The lads in the RAF police have been taking something of a beating recently." (The pub brawling had improved but had not gone away altogether.)

"Yessss?" Alarm bells had started to ring but Dad hadn't yet worked out where this was going.

"I want you to train the lads in self-defence – starting tomorrow morning."

Too late, the full consequences of his bragging dawned on him and Dad tried to back-track. "But…but…I'm really n-n-not that good," he stammered.

The CO regarded the six feet two, broad-shouldered, young man in front of him. 'Stout fellow,' he thought. This was just the sort of modest, quietly spoken, but evidently deadly, sort of chap that was needed for the job. He had no time for idle boasters. "Nine O'clock sharp in the gym," he said, dismissing Dad with a satisfied smile and a wave of the hand.

That night my extremely agitated father was up till the crack of dawn, frantically turning the pages of '*Judo for Beginners*' with one hand whilst throwing my even more agitated mother around the room with the other.

"That one seemed a little better didn't it, Dear?" he would ask hopefully as she crashed to the floor yet again.

Worried about the yells, thumps and groans coming from the living room, I woke my five-year-old brother, Jock. "Domestic problems," he yawned. "Best not interfere." With that he rolled over and went back to sleep.

Dawn broke to find Mum still flying through the air, and Dad desperately jotting down the numbers of his more successful pages. As he set out for work that morning, '*Judo for Beginners*' tucked under his trembling arm, he made a haggard figure– but not quite so haggard as Mum.

His first training session went better than expected. With his little judo book secreted at some strategic point in the gymnasium, he lined up the class and impressed them with a deep Japanese-style bow which he'd perfected in front of the mirror that morning. While he had them all bobbing up and down, perfecting their bows, he furtively flicked through the pages of his book and selected a throw. He then called out two likely-looking lads, described the move to them, and told them to get on with it while he watched to see the result. Unsurprisingly, it was a disaster, so he ridiculed their efforts and, as the whole class were doing fifty press-ups each as a punishment for their incompetence, he quickly consulted his little book again. He then called out two more hopefuls to try the now slightly modified throw. This process would carry on until some semblance of a throw had been made or the class were just too exhausted to do any more press-ups.

Over the weeks, in between the punishment press-ups, his students pounded each other in the vain belief that the useless techniques they were being taught could somehow be made to work with months of hard practice. They may not have learned much judo but, with all the press-ups he had them doing, they'd got arms like tree trunks and were fit as fiddles by the time he'd finished with them. In this way he actually managed to produce some results and his pupils were eager for the next pub brawl to erupt so they could put to use their new-found 'skills'.

At this point, Granny became seriously ill and Dad requested a posting back to Northern Ireland, so we could be near her. In recognition of his fine work with discipline and with training the RAF police, this was reluctantly granted and we were already on our way home to Belfast when Dad's lads, brimming with new-found confidence, burst into a notorious trouble spot and were promptly ejected again through every available window.

"Was für ein feiner großer Junge," said the man at the airport as we caught the plane. "Auf wiedersehen."

"Alf Beederbain," I called back in fluent German.

CHAPTER 3

THE UNRELENTING STRUGGLE

It was Easter-time when we arrived back in Belfast. We were fussed over and spoilt by all our relatives who had been sadly deprived of our wonderful company for the greater part of our lives, bless them. The Easter eggs flew in from all directions. They lasted us for several weeks despite the voracious rate at which we consumed them and the fact that Harold took his to bed with him and they all melted – much to Mum's delight. We took that as the norm for Easter, and my brothers and I were deeply disappointed with the egg-count every year after that magnificent munch-in of 1963.

I was now four years-old, bilingual in one language, and had that easy air of self-assurance only found in someone who has never done or experienced anything in life. Nothing that I was to do in the next few years did anything to dent that confidence, especially when I discovered that the locals understood the English language. The need to break any more of my limbs in order to get my gnashers round and ice-cream was thus removed.

Dad had now settled in at RAF Ballykelly and, when our supply of Easter eggs had finally been depleted, we moved up to nearby Limavady. We made our home in a caravan on old George's farm on the Roe Mill Road. I thought it was great because it had bunk beds. After a few battles, tantrums and complex negotiations (that had to go to arbitration at M.U.M.) I managed to steal the top bunk from under (or should I say 'over') big brother Jock.

I should have realised that he would not take these sleeping arrangements lying down. I mysteriously started falling out of bed in the middle of the night, so I was relegated to the relative safety of the bottom bunk while Jock ascended to the top of the ladder. He always regarded this position as his birth right and to this day I have a sneaking suspicion that he had been creeping up to the top bunk while I was asleep, and pushing me out. To make matters worse, I had to share the bottom bunk with the villain who had stolen away my Mum's attention – Harold.

Sleeping on the bottom bunk was not without its dangers. My parents were soon awoken, not by the usual crash of me falling out of bed, but of my terrified scream of, "SNAAAAKE!" Jock was dangling a tie down from the top bunk. Having assured me that St. Patrick had driven all the snakes out of Ireland well before bedtime, Mum managed to persuade me to climb back into bed. I punched Harold just to make sure he realised that I had not really been scared at all.

On another occasion I decided to sneak out of bed and have a crafty run around, even though Mum and Dad were still awake. Unfortunately, Harold had already been up, shat in the potty and then, without pushing it back under the bed, gone off to find some toilet paper.

I stepped right in it.

Disgusted, I ran around in circles yelling and shouting. This was a poor idea as Harold's excrement was spread in a wide circle around the room (not for the last time). Also it attracted Dad's attention.

When he arrived in the doorway, turned on the light, and saw shitty little footprints everywhere, he went ballistic. He had a policy of never hitting us when he was angry, so he took out his frustration by kicking the bed instead.

Mum, who was in the kitchen peeling spuds, turned around when she heard the commotion. All she could see was my father kicking something, and she could hear me screaming. She put two and two together and made five. She came running into the bedroom, knife still in hand, determined to protect her little boy from this madman who had previously been her loving husband.

Out of the corner of his eye, Dad caught a glimpse of this madwoman, who had previously been his adoring wife, coming at him with a knife. He reacted instinctively and threw her across the room where she landed in a heap in the corner. Horrified at what he'd done, he tried to get over to help her up, but I thought he was going to attack her so I leapt on him, wrapped myself around his leg, and sank my teeth in. As Dad slowly and painfully dragged himself over to my sobbing mother, yelling above the gnashing noises coming from his leg, for me to get off him, Harold finished wiping his bum and, oblivious to the chaos his bowels had caused, walked past this loving family scene, slipped into bed and went back to sleep.

The next day I expected a beating for chewing on Dad's leg, but he said that I'd done the right thing, trying to protect my mum, and he gave me a penny instead. I saw Harold looking enviously at the penny and then hungrily at Dad's leg, trying to work out if the trick would work for him as well. Wisely he thought better of it.

Jock started school soon after we moved to Limavady. After all Dad's stories of sex, drugs and rock and roll (Dad had been to Public School) he had been looking forward to it immensely, but he came home with a face like a battered bulldog. With each passing day he became more and more quiet and withdrawn. He was being bullied.

Dad had made the mistake of ignoring his natural instincts, and allowed Mum to bring Jock up to be nice, stick up for the underdog, and not to do anything nasty such as fighting.

The scene was set then. Jock arrived at the rough-and-ready Northern Irish school, with a fairly posh 'Forces English' accent that he'd picked up in Germany, polished off with an odd German twang. The local kids gathered around in amazement to poke and prod him and listen to the way he said, 'Would you mind not doing that, my good man?' or 'GOTT IN HIMMEL!' in response to a particularly penetrating prod. He made things worse for himself by trying to stick up for underdogs and so fell foul of the bullies as well as the casual pokers and prodders.

Harold and I used to walk up a path known as the 'Double Ditch', to see Jock in the school playground at lunch times. He would come up to the railings and wave cheerfully at us across the street (we weren't allowed to cross the road) then he'd go back to be bullied again.

Jock told me that school was great, and I only found out what he was going through when I overheard our parents talking about it. I was furious. No one was going to bully my big brother and get away with it.

I found out who the main culprit was; a big, nasty lad, all of seven years-old. That afternoon, around kicking out time at school, I slipped out of the caravan. Mum soon realised I was missing and went looking for me. She found me halfway up the Double Ditch, hiding in the bushes, toy car in hand, waiting to ambush the bully as he passed by. She dragged me home and put me under house arrest until further notice.

Meanwhile, Dad decided the time had come to teach us to fight. He showed us how to make a fist and punch through an object. I went straight out to practice and walloped the first kid unfortunate enough to walk by. It worked. He fell flat on his back then ran off squealing. In a state of euphoria, I ran back home to look for Harold so that I could practice some more.

After further boxing lessons from Dad, Jock was packed off to school on the Monday with strict instructions to stand up for himself and not to worry if he got into trouble with the teachers. He arrived home that evening looking pretty pleased with himself.

Dad could hardly contain his excitement. "What happened at school today, Jock?" he asked expectantly.

A look of indignation crossed Jock's flushed face. "A

34

boy pished on my leg in the toilets," he said.

"And what did you do, son?" Dad asked eagerly, waiting with bated breath for the gory details of Jock's first fight. "What did you do when he pished on your leg?"

Jock looked puzzled, as if the answer was obvious. "I took it out of the way," he said.

Dad gave up on a hopeless cause but Harold and I decided to help out. We turned up outside the school at lunchtimes, lobbing bricks and stones at anyone that came near Jock in the playground. Unfortunately, as well as keeping the bullies at bay, this tactic did tend to make it difficult for him to make friends. Also, as our aim was not as good as our intentions, Jock used to go back to class after lunch-break, covered in cuts and bruises where stray stones had hit him. This made the teachers suspect that he was being bullied and so the problem was sorted out.

On the subject of self-defence, Dad, still flushed with the imagined success of his period as a judo sensei in Germany, decided to start a judo club in Limavady. He managed to persuade the RAF that it would be a good public relations exercise to set up a joint Forces/civilian club and, armed with a grant from them, he teamed up with a local judo man to found the 'Ken-cho-kai'.

Ken-cho-kai is Japanese for 'Dog-leap Club'. This may sound like a strange name for a judo club, but in Irish it translates as 'Limavady Club'. The town of Limavady was named after a famous historical event in the area. A local chieftain had lost a battle and was trapped with his back to the River Roe as his enemies closed in on him. His faithful wolfhound had no intention of being captured and so, taking a run-up at the river, it leapt right over to the other side and stood waiting for its master. Taking heart from this, the chieftain made a giant leap at the fast-flowing river, landed in the middle, and was swept away, never to be seen again. (I may have got the details slightly wrong). The town that eventually sprung up on the site took the name 'Dog leap', or 'Limavady', after the event.

The chief instructor at the Ken-cho-kai, was a bull of a man called, Uncle Bill. That's what we called him anyway. Most people just called him 'Sir' and hurried past with their eyes lowered. His shoulders were so broad that he would sit all four of us on them, two to a shoulder.

"Four of you?" I hear you saying. Yes. Another brother had been born while we were in Limavady – but that was yet to come.

Dad borrowed an RAF lorry, and set off with Uncle Bill and the grant money to buy the equipment they needed to set up the judo club. On their way back they pulled out of a junction, and into a gap in a convoy of army trucks that was travelling down the main road. Dad eventually turned off onto the Roe Mill Road, and pulled up outside the judo club, a mile down the street. When they climbed out of the cab, they found a line of army trucks parked behind them. They'd all been blindly following the lorry in front, and the Pied Piper had led them down a blind alley. Uncle Bill and Dad were delighted, and giggled away as they unloaded their goods, as half a dozen confused-looking army drivers frantically consulted their maps.

They set up the judo club in the loft of a derelict old

building across the road from our caravan, laying down some thin sponge mats and stretching canvas over them. Where the rest of the grant money went, only God, Dad and the local barman know. All the local hard-nuts were soon turning up and they happily smashed each other around, four or five nights a week, then piled back to our caravan for the drink, the grub and the crack. That was back in the days when crack was a mixture of blarney and wit rather than a mixture of cocaine and talcum powder – but you wouldn't have thought so if you'd seen them. The caravan used to literally rock with their laughter.

Jock and I, who were kept awake most nights by their racket (Harold slept through it), decided that we wanted to take up judo. We didn't know what it was but, judging by the constant laugher, we thought it must be hilarious, whatever it was. Dad bought us each a little judo suit (which made us giggle a little, but not much) and promised to take us along to the club. First though, he taught Jock how to break-fall, with hours spent rolling off the settee and slapping the floor with his arms. (I was excused as Dad judged that I'd already had enough practice from falling off the top bunk every night.)

The time finally arrived when we were allowed to set foot in the mysterious judo club. Shaking with excitement, we were led up various stairways in the dark, spooky, derelict old building, then pushed up through a trapdoor into the loft where the practice was held. By this time we were both terrified and having our first doubts about how hilarious judo might be.

As people started flinging us around the mat, I stole a

glance at Jock. If my eyes and ears didn't deceive me, he wasn't laughing either.

What was it that everyone found so amusing about this controlled thuggery?

Jock hit the ground again and, as I looked at his miserable expression and drooping cheeks, I admit I had to suppress a giggle. Maybe that was it? Bouncing off yet another wall, I shelved that idea. Jock was watching me with a semi-smirk on his face but the truth was we still weren't having much fun. Next time I hit the floor, someone started to strangle me. No! That wasn't very amusing either. This was followed by a painful arm-lock. I yelled – but not in delight. We crawled home, battered, bruised and confused.

It was not until the following evening that I discovered how much fun judo could be. Dad dragged us, kicking and screaming, back to the judo club. He was impressed by our enthusiasm but said we should wait until we got there before kicking, and that we should time the screams to coincide with the kicks. (Apparently it focuses all your energy into the blow). Uncle Bill set up a judo contest between Jock and me. By this time Jock, who was a gentle soul at heart, had lost all interest in judo and accepted that he would never get the joke, whatever it was. My competitive spirit however, was roused at the thought of a fight, and I flew at him in a determined manner. Jock easily wrestled me to the ground but I remembered one of the holds that Uncle Bill had shown us and I twisted around and clamped that on him. Hell or high water could not have shaken me off, never mind Jock's half-hearted attempt at a struggle. I clung on like a limpet and, thirty seconds later, arose victorious and beaming.

Uncle Bill presented me with a medal that, for some strange reason, had a horse's head on it. It must have been a horse racing medal that he'd found lying around and had recycled for the occasion. No matter. I loved that medal (my first) and I was hooked. I've been betting on the horses ever since.

I was proud of beating Jock in my first judo contest, but each night the judo guys were still coming back to our place and still laughing all night – and I still didn't get it. What was so funny about judo? Then one weekend I was playing in our garden when Farmer George's grandnephew appeared. He was older and bigger than me and decided it would be a good idea to push me around – literally. As he pushed, I caught him by the lapels, put one foot on his belly and rolled backwards, throwing him over my head with tomoenagi - a stomach throw. He hurtled through the air, landed in some thorn bushes, then ran off screaming.

Laugh!!? I nearly shat myself. As I rolled around holding my sides I finally realised what the others already knew. Judo is a real scream. I was hooked and have been ever since.

Back in the caravan my giggles were cut short by a loud rapping on the door. Dad opened it and there, all flaring nostrils and jutting chin, stood Farmer George, his reluctant and sheepish-looking grandnephew in tow.

"Your Jock beat up my lad," growled old George.

"Jock," called Dad, beaming at this unexpected news, "Did you hit this boy?"

The obvious pride in Dad's voice quickly turned to disappointment when Jock denied any involvement in the administration of the beating.

"He's lying..." began old George.

Dad cut him off. "John," he called.

"It was your Jock!" spluttered George.

Dad ignored him. "John," he called again.

"Yes, Dad?"

"Did you beat up this boy?" he asked sternly.

"Yes, Dad," I said proudly.

"Good lad," he whispered, patting me on the head. He raised his voice. "And can you tell us why?"

"Because he was bullying me, Dad," I stated firmly.

Old George looked at me and then at his nephew. It didn't escape his notice that I was half his size. "Is this true," he roared at the boy. "Was it John you were fighting with?"

He admitted that it was and was dragged off by the ear by the angry old farmer.

The appearance of Farmer George's grandnephew on the scene, coincided with the disappearance of any toys we left outside. This mystery, if never actually solved, was finally brought to a satisfactory conclusion when Jock and I decided to go climbing on Farmer George's barn. Straying anywhere near this rickety old structure was strictly against the rules, being banned both by our parents and by Farmer George himself. It was therefore irresistible. After intense negotiations, I finally persuaded Jock to join me on a clandestine expedition to the barn. I would have gone on my own but what's the point of being naughty if no-one else knows about it. It's the team spirit engendered by being naughty together that makes it all worthwhile. That's why we have cabinet government in this country.

Jock and I shinned up an old drainpipe and edged our way up to the top of the barn roof. We played a game of dare to see which one of us could walk the furthest along the top ridge without falling off. Jock won.

I slipped, slid down the far side of the roof, dangled for a few seconds by one hand from the eaves gutter, then plummeted earthwards. Luckily my fall was broken by the ground. I rolled backwards on impact and slammed into the barn door which burst open. There, piled up just inside, were our missing toys. Instinctively knowing that direct action would be more effective than going through the proper channels (i.e. telling Dad and receiving a thrashing for going near the barn), we collected them up and took them home.

Jock, of course, couldn't keep his trap shut, and admitted what had happened.

"So that's where the toys disappeared to," smiled Mum.

"He's an eccentric old sod," laughed Dad as he set about us with his belt.

We didn't know what 'eccentric' meant, but he was right. Old George was a real character. He was getting on in years and, after a number of accidents, his doctor advised him that he was too old to ride about on his beloved bicycle. His eyesight wasn't what it used to be, and he was becoming a danger both to himself and to the community at large. Old George surprised everyone by taking the doctor's advice and selling the bike.

The next day he bought a car.

The ensuing mayhem must have touched on the lives of the greater part of the population of Limavady, if not of the Province as a whole. The local mothers would run out when they heard his car approach. It had a very distinctive sound to it, very similar to Farmer George's hacking cough. They would gather up their children and any stray waifs in the area, then race for cover. I remember on many occasions, having been rudely interrupted at play and dragged into the relative safety of a neighbour's caravan, cowering behind closed doors and listening to the sound of dustbins being scattered as Old George parked his car.

On the first day he had his car, before his reputation as a driver had spread far and wide, Mum and her friend foolishly accepted a lift home from him late one evening. After a few hundred yards, terrified out of their wits, they managed to persuade him to slow down and, as he braked for a tight corner, they flung open the doors and rolled out into the night.

To be fair to Old George, the wide open, flapping doors caught his attention and he noticed that Mum and her friend were missing. He stopped and got out to look for them. They hid in the bushes until he gave up the search. They then walked the five miles home arriving, shaken but unhurt, a good ten minutes before Old George came spluttering into the yard, scattering the dustbins yet again. From then on they caught the bus.

Old George, when he was not farming or terrorising the neighbourhood in his car, spent most of his spare time collecting antique clocks, and he prided himself on his unscrupulous eye for a bargain. He had a house full of clocks and his wife, who did not share her husband's passion, leant one to our neighbour, Willy, when his broke.

A few weeks later, Old George, along with my Mum and Dad, was at Willy's caravan enjoying a game of poker. He spotted the clock. Immediately recognising it as a valuable piece (but not as one of his own) he switched into bargain-hunting mode.

"That's a nice clock you've got there, Willy," George said nonchalantly. "Where did you get it?"

Realising that Old George thought he might be on to a nice little bargain, Willy decided to play him along. "Oh, that auld thing? It's just a piece of junk I picked up at a jumble sale."

George was hooked. "If you're thinking of getting rid of it, let me know," he said.

"Why?" asked Willy, all innocence. "Is it worth something?"

"No, no, not at all," Old George cut in quickly. "It's worthless. I just like the look of it, that's all."

He eyed Willy, weighing up how much he could do him for. "I'll tell you what," said George, stroking his stubbly chin, "I'm feeling generous. I'll give you a fiver for it."

"Done!" cried Willy, spitting in his hand and clasping Old George's greedy mitt in his own.

'You have been,' thought George as he hurried homewards, five pounds lighter but with the valuable clock tucked safely under his arm. He couldn't wait to tell his wife about his bargain.

"Look what I've bought," he cackled in delight, flourishing the clock in front of her face. "It's worth a fortune, and that dim Willy let me have it for a fiver!"

"YOU AULD FOOL," she yelled. "YOU'VE BOUGHT YOUR OWN BLOODY CLOCK!"

It nearly killed him.

But enough about Farmer George for the moment. I was now four years old and was about to have yet another sibling foisted on me by my mother.

"Have you never heard of contraception, woman," I scolded her.

The real reason that Mum kept getting pregnant (apart from the obvious) was that she wanted a daughter and, no matter how many sons she had to pop out before she had one, have one she would – but not this time.

Another son it was and, being imaginative, they decided to call *him* Harold as well. Harold, was named after a great uncle on Dad's side of the family, but Harold, was named for one on Mum's side, so they assumed it would cause no confusion. They were wrong.

Little Harold was born in Limavady, following yet another massive push from Mum. She was a terrible shot. We landed everywhere - England, Ireland and Scotland. The birth coincided with me starting school, and it was with a sense of shock and betrayal that I regarded this latest interloper when I arrived home full of excited tales of my first day at school, only to be ignored as everyone fussed around the baby.

I was terrified to go to school the next day in case I

arrived home to find yet another one waiting for me. Each day I hurried back, full of trepidation, searching around for any tell-tale signs, but Mum seemed to be content with just the one baby for the moment, and I gradually settled down.

Little Harold was a quiet baby. He kept to his cot and didn't seem to pose any real threat to me. I kept a wary eye on him but decided not to punch him. I was mellowing in my old age.

School suited me. There were plenty of other kids to fight with, sandpits to pee in, and paint to splash about in the classroom. We sang hymns around a grand piano, stuffed odd-shaped blocks of wood into odd-shaped holes, and stood on one leg with our arms in the air, pretending to be trees. Within a month I had learned all I needed to know to see me through the rest of my life.

Despite this, I was to spend the next twenty-odd years in the education system, learning things in order to get to the next level of education, then forgetting them as I was taught the new things necessary to get to the next level before forgetting them, and so on. This education thing earned me little pieces of paper which, when produced at interviews later in life, got me jobs, even though I couldn't remember a thing I'd learned in order to get the pieces of paper. The employers knew this, but didn't care. The important thing was having the piece of paper. The knowledge seemed to be irrelevant.

It's a very strange system. Why don't they just give kids the pieces of paper after their first month of school, then they could leave and do something productive like cleaning chimneys (if we still had coal fires); tie broken threads under looms (if we still had a textile industry); go down the pits (if we still had a mining industry); or go to sea as cabin boys (if we still had a merchant marine).

Okay, I'm beginning to see why they have an education system. There are no jobs for young people anymore. I've heard rumours that the Government is planning to put up the school-leaving age to sixty-seven, in order to achieve full employment. Think of all the job-seekers allowance it would save!

Harold started school the year after me. He arrived back home one day, walked in through the French Windows, and greeted Mum with our usual home-coming cry of, "Mummy, I'm HOOOooommeAAAGGHH!" (Well the 'HOOOooomme' was usual, but the, 'AAAGGHH', certainly wasn't.)

Mum hurried in from the kitchen and found him lying on the floor, semi-conscious and mumbling to himself. Later in life, this would be a common occurrence, but this was a first and she was concerned. But she could find no explanation.

The next day, I arrived home from school. I took no chances with the hexed French Windows and instead climbed the breeze block steps to the front door, and shouted, "Mummy, I'm HOOOooommeAAAGGHH!"

'Not again,' thought Mum, quickly spinning around to where she'd heard my cry. The open door flapped in the breeze, but there was no sign of me. She ran to the door and found me lying flat on my back in the middle of the garden, mumbling incoherently to myself.

Mum and Dad decided to have the caravan exorcised.

There seemed to be some sort of poltergeist that was triggered by the words, "Mummy, I'm home." Fortunately, before they made fools of themselves, they found the 'lucky' horseshoe that had fallen off the wall above the French Windows and hit Harold on the head before rolling under a chair. (This is the sort of luck that Harold has had for most of his life.) Little Harold, who had only mastered a few words, pointed at the horseshoe and said, "Hurt Harold." He'd obviously seen the whole thing, but couldn't explain it to anyone.

My experience was put down to either a freak gust of wind as I opened the door, or to a regression in Jock to his baby bowel-movements, either of which would have had the power to catapult me halfway across the garden.

They may have been right but, to this day, I never say, "Mummy, I'm home," out loud. It is with considerable trepidation that I've even written it.

While on the subject of poltergeists, I may as well tell you about some of the strange goings-on in Limavady, where the fairies and the little people were up to their tricks. There is a path leading from Roe Mill Road, down through the woods to the River Roe. We knew the path as 'The Fairy Lane'. On a summer's evening we would walk down The Fairy Lane with our Grandparents and Uncle Hugh and Auntie May. We'd run ahead, finding sweets and coins that the fairies had left out for us along the length of the lane. Occasionally we'd find a packet of cigarettes but Grampa insisted they were meant for him. We objected because we knew that big folks can't see the little people so we argued that the cigs must have been meant for us. Uncle Hugh agreed with us, but Grampa was not to be persuaded, and we reluctantly handed them over. On the way back we would buy lollipops then, just before bedtime, we'd run out and plant the empty lollipop sticks in the garden. When we awoke in the morning the lollipop sticks had grown into real lollipops.

Funnily enough, now that I think about it, these strange goings-on only occurred when Grampa and Uncle Hugh were visiting. I now realise what was happening. Those two obviously had a way with the little people after all.

These encounters with the other world must have had an effect on out parents, both regular churchgoers, because they developed an increasing interest in the supernatural – but then again it was the sixties, and everybody was a bit loopy. They somehow reconciled this with their religion, and never made human sacrifices – much to my disappointment.

They were interested in all things that may or may not go bump in the night and were always concerned that the good guys on Jesus' side should get the upper hand over the n'er-do-wells of Auld Nick's eleven. Myself, I always had more sympathy with the old drunk we used to see in Belfast. He was terrified of walking past the graveyard and was obviously in fear for his mortal soul. He'd hurry past, hedging his bets by shouting, "God's good. God's good. And the Devil's not a bad old fellah either."

Their main interest in this sort of thing came when we were living in Scotland amongst like-minded witch-burners in our church and local community. When we moved on to England, where the majority of the populace has about as much religious fervour as a Church of England bishop, they became less and less interested in matters spiritual – or temporal for that matter. Now that doesn't leave a lot, you may be thinking, but these times were still to come and, meanwhile, I was busy learning to ride a bicycle in Limavady.

I had made one previous attempt to ride a bike when we were in Germany. Jock had been given one for his birthday and I decided to sneak out and have a go on it when he wasn't looking. Dad spotted me clambering awkwardly on and, realising that I would soon fall off, he set off as fast as his legs would carry him – to fetch his camera. His latest hobby was photography, and he was not about to let the small matter of a few possible broken bones to his second-born come between him and a good photograph.

He emerged too late for the action photo he had dreamed of. I was already lying in a heap, with the bicycle on top of me, crying my eyes out. He gently lifted me into a sitting position (in order to get a better camera angle), rubbed me reassuringly on my tear-streaked cheek with his light metre, then snapped my distress for posterity.

That had been some time ago, but I still checked to make sure he hadn't got his camera before I agreed to set out with him to learn to ride a bike. I wouldn't have put it past him to push me straight down a hill in order to get a picture of me flying over the handlebars. Satisfied that his intentions were honourable, I set of for my first lesson with my father, a bicycle, and high aspirations.

Dad held the back of the saddle to support me and, as I

peddled, he instructed me to move the handlebars to and fro to keep my balance. My time in Germany, where the emphasis is on blindly following orders, and my own natural inclination to take everything literally, combined with my youthful exuberance, led to a flurry of movement as I pedalled like a whirling dervish, my arms a blur as I whipped the handlebars back and forth. I had soon out-distanced my father who had to let go when he couldn't keep up.

The locals screamed and dived for cover when they saw me coming, thinking that Old George was back on his bike again. I did not disappoint. I scattered the dustbins as the younger cats, which did not remember Farmer George's cycling days, scurried for the safer hiding places already occupied by their older and wiser brethren. Dad arrived as I lay in a heap surrounded by bin lids and rubbish. He produced a well-concealed camera from his coat pocket and happily snapped away.

When I'd finally staggered to my feet, ignoring Dad's pleas to watch the birdie, he plonked me straight back on the bike with instructions not to move the handlebars from side to side like I'd been doing. This seemed to do the trick and I was doing well until I reached a corner. Remembering Dad's orders not to move the handlebars, I ploughed straight on into a brick wall. Old George himself had appeared by this time, determined to give me the benefit of his experience, but on seeing this, he declared that I could ride as well as the next fellah and disappeared back indoors leaving Dad clicking away on his camera.

By the end of the day, battered and bruised, I had

mastered the noble art of cycling, and thus achieved that extra freedom that the mobility of the bicycle brings to children. The world was becoming a smaller place already, even though it now seemed a bigger one to me.

In line with my policy of taking everything literally (especially if it was to my advantage to do so) I decided to make the most of the situation when, just before bedtime, Dad told Jock and me to get out of his sight. It was only a small caravan so, in order to get out of his sight, it seemed only reasonable to leave altogether. We played in the garden for a while but were concerned that he still might be able to see us, so Jock suggested that we play further down the road to make sure we didn't break Dad's orders.

I was impressed. Surprised but impressed. Jock was at last beginning to use his not inconsiderable intellect in a devious and underhand manner. We could have an adventure and it was all Dad's fault, so we couldn't get in trouble. (I would have gone anyway, but Jock needed to convince himself.)

A mile or so down the road we found a telegraph pole which was held in place by four hawsers. Immediately behind this was a stone wall, about five feet in height. Climbing onto the wall, we'd grab a hawser and slide down to the ground, then clamber back up again and repeat the process. Now, as you can imagine, this varied pastime did not occupy persons of our high intellect for very long and so, two hours later, we trudged back home. At least Jock trudged. I was so tired that he had to give me a piggy-back ride. This simple act was to save us from a beating.

Meanwhile, night had fallen. (Why is it that the sun

51

sets, but poor old night always falls? Still, the day breaks so I suppose it's swings and roundabouts really.) The hue-and-cry had gone up an hour earlier when Mum had gone to check on us in bed and we were nowhere to be seen. After giving Dad a tongue-lashing when he admitted he'd told me, of all people, to get out of his sight, Mum raised the countryside. All the neighbours were out dragging the woods and beating the rivers (it was Ireland after all). They were beginning to despair when Jock staggered into view with me fast asleep on his back. We looked such a sorry sight that the neighbours laughed, Mum cried with relief, and even Dad couldn't bring himself to wake me up for a thrashing. Jock even took on something of a heroic mantle for managing to bring me home in my unconscious state. With Harold, in years to come, this would be a common occurrence, but this was a first and we got away with it.

We both learned from this and from then on, in awkward or dangerous situations, Jock attempted something heroic, and I went to sleep. This double act saved us from hidings on several occasions. One example is when, a few years later, we accidentally started a forest fire in Scotland.

I know what you're thinking. How did we start a fire in Scotland when we were living in Ireland? Was Jock still having trouble with his bowels? Had Harold flung aside an empty jam jar on a sunny day? Had someone said, 'strike a light' to me at an inappropriate moment? Had Mum fired out another baby? The answer to all those questions is, yes, but that is not how the fire started.

Following in Dad's itchy footsteps, we had moved to Scotland. We were living in Scone, the place where Scottish kings used to be crowned on the Stone of Destiny (which the Scots had nicked from Ireland) before the English, under Edward 1 of 'Braveheart' fame, stole it and moved it to Westminster Abbey and crowned their own kings on it. The Scots recently pinched it back but proved just as untrustworthy as their southern cousins and sent it to Edinburgh, not Scone – its 'rightful' resting place. The Irish are still waiting for the Scots to return it to them. If the Scots finally show some moral conscience and give the Stone of Destiny back to the Irish, then Ireland will eventually have to give it back to Israel, as The Stone of Destiny is believed to be the biblical Stone of Jacob, originally taken from Bethal, modern day Beitin in the occupied West Bank. The Israelis will then have to give it back to Jordan, as the West Bank is really theirs. The Jordanians will probably have to give it to the Palestinians if they are given the West Bank as a Palestinian homeland. Babylon probably has a claim to it as well, as they conquered Israel back in the day, as did Rome – so maybe it should be taken to Italy.

Perhaps it's best to just leave well alone and not pander to nationalists demanding that this or that be returned to its 'rightful' owners from days of antiquity.

We were actually living just up the road in the slightly busier New Scone. Our house was surrounded on three sides by woodland, so it was the ideal place to bring up children provided that you had a big family and didn't mind losing one or two.

One inauspicious day we appropriated a sausage each from the fridge, slipped a matchbox into Harold's pocket (Jock and I didn't want to risk being caught with matches) and sped away on our bicycles. We met up with our friends in the woods behind the scout hut, with an illicit barbecue on the agenda. This was at the tail-end of a long, hot summer, and the fact that the preceding months had been as dry as a badger's arson was not on our minds as we lit a fire for our sausage-fest, but circumstances were against us. In January of that year, hurricane-force winds had swept the country and had uprooted a number of trees in the area. These large firs had been left at various angles, some being cradled in the branches of their more upright brother pines.

The scene was set then. The trees lying at an angle made for easy climbing, and the hot, dry summer made for easy burning. As our friends were piling wood on the fire, Jock and I half walked and half climbed up the angled trunk of one of the uprooted trees. We had reached the point where our tree became entangled in the branches of an upright one when we noticed our 'friend' Liz, standing thirty feet beneath us and holding a burning stick in her grubby mitt.

"I'm gonna burn you alive!" she shouted happily as she thrust the burning rod into the lower branches of the upright tree. Her laugh stopped abruptly as the tree went up like a torch.

We could see Andy, the oldest and most sensible one there, running around in circles beneath us, trying to organise some sort of fire-fighting effort. "Quick!" he yelled. "Somebody pish on it!"

James tried, but it evaporated quicker than he could pee, and he had to tuck it away again before he ended up with a burning rod of his own.

Meanwhile, Jock had seen the tree in front of us turn into a raging inferno. He turned and tried to run back down the sloping trunk we were on, blundered into me as I stood frozen like a rabbit caught in headlights, and sent us both tumbling out of the tree. We crashed down through the branches for a heavy landing, especially for Jock as I landed on top of him, but this probably saved our lives because, seconds later, the tree we'd just been in went up in smoke.

With James's gallant attempt to extinguish the flames having failed, and a forest fire rapidly beginning to take hold, we abandoned our fire-fighting attempts and turned to Plan B. We ran like buggery.

Stupidly, because we didn't want to be seen, we ran off through the woods, just keeping ahead of the fire. When we reached home we realised that we'd left our bicycles beside the scout hut. We had to go back.

We walked the long way round by the road and, when we eventually reached the scene of the crime, the place was packed with fire engines, fire-fighters and noisy onlookers. The blaze had spread to several other trees and it was all the fire-fighters could do to contain it.

Luckily for us, all eyes were on the fire and no one noticed us as we slunk in, picked up our bicycles, and slunk out again.

We tried to act nonchalantly when we arrived home, but our smoke-reeking clothes and Jock's singed eyebrows gave us away. I feared the worst but then stood entranced as Jock told the heroic tale of how, with no thought for his own safety, he had thrown himself through the flames to drag me out of the tree and had then cushioned my fall with his own body. My, "but...but's" were silenced with a couple of surreptitious but well-aimed kicks to the shins, and Jock's story carried the day. Dad praised his bravery and quick thinking in saving his younger brother, and we escaped a beating.

The fire-fighters eventually brought the blaze under control and saved the scout hut from the flames. But the scouts were banned from lighting campfires thereafter. The sweet refrain of, 'Ging gang gooley gooley' was heard no more in one small corner of Britain.

But that lay in the future. Meanwhile, back in Limavady, Dad was becoming increasingly bemused by the fact that the locals were even more eccentric than him. This had never happened to him before, and indeed it never happened after, and he was not going to take it lying down. He was determined to put matters right and reclaim his rightful place at the top of the eccentric hall of fame.

Once again enlisting the help of his partners-in-crime, the RAF, who were always ready to put men and money into any operation that made no sense, he purchased the appropriate equipment, hand-picked an unenthusiastic team made available from the guard-house, and set off to cross Ireland by canoe. The facts that he couldn't swim, and that Ireland is mainly made of earth, not water, deterred him not at all.

Months later they returned in triumph, having walked across much of Ireland carrying canoes whilst vainly trying to find rivers, lakes or puddles to paddle in. In some of the remoter and more backward parts of the country, the passing of this strange, canoe-carrying cult, led to a deep-rooted belief that The Deluge was soon to come again. Whole communities took to staggering around the countryside with canoes on their heads and berating the unbelievers who doubted that the second Great Flood was imminent.

When the pilgrim returned and fought his way through the Press, who were besieging our caravan for a glimpse of this latter-day Noah, the strange, bearded apparition introduced itself to us as our father. Jock, being slightly older and wiser than the rest of us, recognised him immediately. Harold and I recognised him when he took the canoe off his head. Little Harold, as was his policy, refused to recognise him at all until he was given a present – which he duly was.

We were all given presents, and then an attempt was made to line us up for a family photograph with the home-coming hero, both for our own album and for the local press. The attempt was doomed to failure. We had just been reunited with our long-lost father and had been given new toys to play with. Standing still and posing for the camera was the last thing on our minds.

Little Harold, the youngest, would not stop running around and kicking his new ball. He was furious when, in a badly thought out plan to make him stand still, it was taken from him. He promptly flung himself on the ground and bawled his head off. I was furious because Harold had been given a toy boat while I had been given a clown car. (If it had been the other way around, I'd have wanted the car.) So I ran off to fetch *my* toy boat. Jock was furious because he took his responsibilities as big brother very seriously. As usual he was trying to organise us and as usual he was failing dismally. Mum was furious because the press photographers were trampling down her flowers as they moved around the garden desperately trying to get us all in the frame at the same time. Harold was furious because I eventually returned with a bigger boat than his, *and* my clown car, then posed ready for the snap.

When I say that Harold was furious, that is a slight exaggeration. Harold never got furious at anything. He was, however, slightly miffed and joined us all in a communal look of disgust at Little Harold, who was still screaming the place down as he pined for his beloved, but confiscated, ball. This then, was the happy scene that was finally snapped and captured for posterity in the family album, the local press, and the Flat Earth Society Newsletter.

I was now five years old and had reached a rebellious age. My confidence having been boosted by the 'get out of my sight,' incident, where no beating had been administered, I engaged in an open argument with my father. While the heated debate remained on an intellectual level, I was getting the worst of it, so I decided to hit below the belt.

"I'm going to tell someone your middle name!" I shouted, then stormed out.

Reaching the bottom of the garden, I spotted two little, old women toddling down the road towards me. This was my chance! As they passed by the fence I jumped out and yelled, "My Dad's middle name is…HUMBERT!" They leapt six feet in the air and rounded on me when they eventually landed, cursing like troopers.

I was shocked. I had known it was bad, but not *that* bad. Two prim and proper, little old ladies screaming and swearing at the very mention of that terrible name.

'That showed him,' I thought as I stomped back to the caravan, leaving the old women still chuntering by the roadside. It had been even more successful than I had dared to hope. Triumphant, I marched into the living-room and hit Dad with the lurid details of his downfall. He hit *me* with the flat of his hand. I decided to call it a draw.

Now that the secret of his middle name was out, Dad could no longer show his face in Limavady or at RAF Ballykelly, so he resigned his commission and we moved to Belfast, where he attempted to resume life as an anonymous civilian. I realised then that I had cut off my nose to spite my face. I had been due to have my tonsils out, and was eagerly looking forward to being given ice-cream and a toy motorbike with a sidecar, like Jock after his operation. I was also looking forward to teasing Harold about him still having a full set of useless tonsils stuck in his useless gullet, unlike Jock and me, the hospital heroes. But, because we were moving, my operation was cancelled and my tonsils, older and wiser than they once were, are still with me to this day.

CHAPTER 4

THE END OF THE BEGINNING

Granny M had been ill for a long time. I was envious that she was allowed to stay in bed all day and I used to take advantage of this privilege by climbing in with her whenever we were visiting. Lying in bed she would tell me biblical stories but would spice them up a bit to keep my interest. This led to problems at Sunday school where, like young Jesus with the Pharisees, I would dispute the stories with my teachers (well, maybe not quite like Him - I had a style all of my own.)

"No, no!" I'd scold my Sunday school teacher. "You've got it wrong again. The whale spat out Jonah because he had smelly feet." Or, "Wine? He turned the water into Ribena. Everyone knows that!"

Lazarus had risen from the dead because it was fish fingers for tea that night, and David had slain Goliath after being taunted with, "Sticks and stones can break my bones but words can never hurt me...OUCH!"

I also questioned the wisdom of the so-called, Three Wise Men. Anyone with any sense knows that kids want toys for their birthday. Gold I could just about understand but frankincense was definitely a no-no, and who in their right mind gives a kid myrrh?

They were minor details but ones that I insisted my Sunday school teacher corrected before she was allowed to continue. My granny was always right.

Despite her irreverent attitude towards these bible stories, I think that God must have liked her versions too because, when her time eventually came after a long and painful illness, she smiled, reached out her arms, and passed on peacefully.

Exactly one year after her death, my parents awoke to a strong smell of lavender, Granny's favourite flower. The clock in the living room stopped at the hour of her death, and was never persuaded to start again. Very strange.

Grampa now had a large house all to himself. As Dad had left the RAF and was at a loose end, we packed our bags, piled into our Morris 1000 van, and set off for Belfast, humming the 'Telstar' tune which was all the rage at the time.

It must have been a bit of a culture shock for Grampa to suddenly have four unruly young children living in his house, especially when he was still grieving the loss of his wife, and he could be a bit grumpy and stern at times (mind you, he was a Belfast Presbyterian). But he loved us all dearly and missed us badly when we eventually left. (That's what he told us anyway – it was probably party time on the Lisburn Road. I do have a vague recollection of the sound of a champagne cork popping as we walked out the door.)

I soon endeared myself to him with several little incidents such as the time he took us for a ride in his car. I remember it to this day. It was a blue Ford Consul with orange bench seats and lots of buttons and levers to push and pull, and we thought it was great.

"That boy can sit in the front where I can keep an eye on him," he growled, fixing me with a malevolent stare.

This was a mistake. He could not keep his eye on me all the time as he occasionally had to risk a quick glance at the road to see where he was going. I took advantage of one of these moments and slipped down to the floor where I noticed a lever under the front seat. I looked at it, and it looked at me. I could hear it whispering, "Pull me. Pull me!" So I pulled it.

The seat shot back leaving Grampa's feet flailing in mid-air in a vain attempt to reach the breaks. He was hanging on desperately to the steering wheel with one hand as he frantically tried to swat me with the other. His face turned as orange as the seats, and the air turned as blue as the car. I'd have been deeply shocked if I'd understood a word he said.

I was soon to learn all those words, and a few more besides, when we started at the local primary school. I tried teaching the new ones to Grampa and received a clip round the ear for my attempt to further his education.

Even compared to the one in Limavady, this school was rough and ready, but we were ready to be rough and fitted in alright. At lunchtime we joined in what seemed to be the school sport as everyone had to play unless they had a private quarrel to settle. It was called, 'Cowboys and

Indians.' Half the school would line up on one side of the playground, with the other half facing them. At a 'whoop' from the Indian chief or, more often, a 'yahoo' from the sheriff, a hundred screaming children would charge across the field, belt hell out of each other, then retreat to allow the wounded to crawl to safety before the next bloody, bone-crunching charge.

That first day we innocently lined up in the front row of the Indian Braves, watching with some apprehension the massed ranks of the cowboys. The sheriff always had more recruits than the Indian chief who had to press younger, weaker boys into his service to make up the numbers and give the cowboys something to trample if there were not enough dedicated Indians to go around.

We gallantly stood our ground as the cowboys began their charge, yelling and hollering as they came. As they rapidly closed the gap we looked around at our fellow Braves for support, only to catch sight of the last of them rapidly disappearing around the corner in full retreat. Too late to run, we stood and fought but soon disappeared as well – under a herd of trampling feet.

We were left battered and bruised but we'd done enough to impress the sheriff, and we were invited to join the cowboys. Only Harold refused the offer. I took to the game like a duck to water, once I'd worked out which side to be on, but Jock and I found it very tiring constantly having to help a dishevelled Harold from the field of battle during truces. "But I like Indians," he insisted every time we tried to explain the facts of life to him as we patched him up and dusted him down. He never switched sides.

Although I enjoyed this game, I have never really been one for team sports and so, every other day, I picked a fight with one or another of my classmates. Within a few weeks I had fought and beaten every boy in the class bar two. One was such a little weed that he was beneath my attention; the other was a big, thick lad who'd been kept back a year or two until he got his three R's sorted out. He was above my attention. Discretion being the better part of valour, I ditched my principles and befriended him instead. To assuage my guilty conscience, I told myself that he shouldn't really be in my class anyway, as he was too old.

One boy nearly escaped my attention on two counts, firstly because he was the son of our teacher, Miss Class. I decided to risk the consequences. Secondly, when I informed him of my intentions, he said that I shouldn't hit someone wearing glasses. I pondered this for a minute then reached up and removed them before punching him, as his bottle-top specs looked on reproachfully. I then carefully replaced them, gave him an apologetic pat on the shoulder, and made my way back to class.

The vicar's son also troubled my conscience for a while, not least because he was a friend of mine, but he wasn't on my list of exemptions so, in the end, I had to hit him. Apologising profusely, I smacked him on his parson's nose then went to join in a game of Cowboys and Indians.

Once I had sorted out my classmates my battles were mainly with my teachers, as were those of my brothers. The teachers were a little on the eccentric side, shall we say, and caused us a few problems. Every afternoon, Harold would arrive home from school in tears. It wasn't the Cowboys and Indian's battles that bothered him – after five years with me, he shrugged off a beating as a mere inconvenience. Besides this, Jock and I would protect him and he was never bullied. At home we knocked spots off one another but outside we always stuck up for each other, and woe betide anyone who touched one of the brothers. It was his teacher who was making Harold's life a misery.

Miss Draco was a dragon who, even as dragons go, was somewhat past the first flush of youth, and was looking forward to her telegram from the Queen.

Luckily, I wasn't in her class, Primary One, for long. One day the formidable Miss Class came in and took away four of the older boys. No explanation was given, and we were all curious and speculating on their fate, when the door reopened and in came Miss Class with one of the victims. He was crying his eyes out. Miss Class sat him down with a compassionate slap to the back of the head, and took me instead. Again no explanation. I was terrified but soon found out that all that had happened was that I had been promoted to Primary Two.

Miss Draco was the school pianist so I still had to attend her class for music lessons. Apparently she had been quite accomplished before the senile dementia had set in, but that had been a long time ago. As we dutifully trooped in and began singing like the angels we were, she would hit a barrage of wrong notes then stop and berate us for singing out of tune.

Harold's problem was with his shoes. Every morning, Mum sent him off to school with his shoes on the correct feet, and every afternoon he would return home whimpering, with his shoes on the wrong feet. As soon as he arrived at school, Miss Draco would round on him. "Your shoes are on the wrong feet again you silly boy. Take them off." Then, ignoring his agonised squeals and pleas, she would force them back the wrong way round onto his poor, protesting feet. Our parents eventually complained to the school and Harold's feet gained some respite but, to this day, despite being right-handed, he is left-footed.

The music teacher was eventually forced into retirement after an ill-fated school trip, of which she was 'in charge'. At the end of the visit she climbed back on the bus, counted the children, then told the driver to drive on, which he dutifully did. The problem was that it was the wrong bus and we were left stranded with the teachers from the other school who were frantically trying to find out where all their children had disappeared to.

Jock had more than his fair share of trouble in Mr Porker's class. Mr Porker was the headmaster and was only marginally more senile than Miss Draco, but considerably more violent. He gave poor Jock a hard time.

"What are umpteen thirteens?" he asked him once during an arithmetic lesson. When Jock couldn't answer he shouted, "Thirteen umpteens, boy. The answer is thirteen umpteens." He then made him hold the edge of the desk and caned him across the back of the knuckles – his favourite means of punishment. He dealt out this sort of treatment to poor Jock on a regular basis. When Jock complained, Dad just told him he must have done something to deserve it and that he should behave himself better or he'd get a whack from him as well.

Whenever you are listening to calls for corporal punishment to be brought back in schools, it is worth casting your mind back to some of the sadistic teachers in your own childhood and asking yourself, 'Why should the little buggers get away with it now?' We had to put up with it, so why not them? It would do them a power of good. When I was born we still had capital punishment, and it didn't do *me* any harm. And I wasn't the only one. Most of my best friends were never hanged either.

Before he'd gone up into Mr Porker's class, I'd always volunteered to take any messages to Jock's teachers as an excuse to see, and show off to, my beloved big brother. I'd open the classroom door unannounced, then somersault across the floor to the teacher's desk where I'd dutifully deliver the message, turn and give a big wave to Jock (who'd be trying to hide under his desk in embarrassment) then somersault out again. This behaviour came to an abrupt halt when Jock moved into Mr Porker's class. I somersaulted in as usual, but then found myself somersaulting out again on the end of Mr Porker's size ten boot before I'd even delivered my message, never mind waved to Jock. I learnt my lesson. I've never volunteered for anything since.

Jock was having trouble outside school as well. He was finding out about sectarianism the hard way. His troubles pre-dated 'The Troubles' by a few years and our parents were not prejudiced, so he was not prepared for the outcome of his first solo outing to Saturday morning children's cinema at the Minors ABC.

"We are the boys and girls together, at the Minors ABC," they all sang sweetly during the show. Afterwards they gathered outside to welcome Jock to the gang.

"Which foot do you kick with?" they asked him.

"Mummy says I shouldn't kick," he replied innocently.

"You know what we mean," they growled.

He didn't.

They decided to be blunt. "Are you a Catholic or a Protestant?"

"I don't think so."

"You must be one or the other," they insisted.

"I don't know which."

They were not going to let him get away with it. "Say one," they demanded.

"Which one?"

"JUST SAY ONE!"

He hazarded a guess. "Ehmmm... Protestant?"

They beat him up.

He arrived home, feeling sorry for himself, to find the relatives visiting. "What is a Protestant?" he asked, trying to get to the bottom of this painful mystery.

"A fine, upstanding, God-fearing citizen," came the instant reply.

He decided to play it safe after his earlier treatment. "I'm a Catholic," he declared.

He promptly received another beating.

Not surprisingly, he later became a Buddhist.

"Are you a Catholic Buddhist, or a Protestant Buddhist?" he was once asked.

There are no easy options in Ulster.

My own confrontations with the teaching fraternity began when I entered Primary Three and was faced with the fearsome Miss Munn. She was a fiery, young redhead and we had a love/hate relationship. I loved her and she hated me. "Red hair for danger," I used to shout as she chased me around the classroom, whacking at me with her favourite weapon, a large, wooden ruler.

Her desk was at the front, left corner of the classroom, with the children's desks in three columns of two across the room. In the front desks of column one sat the naughtiest or thickest kids, where Miss Munn could keep an eye on us. The desks stretched away from this, in order of merit, to the far corner at the back of column three where the cleverest and best-behaved little swats sat, safe from the riff-raff of column one – until lunchtime. At lunchtime they would be lined up in the front ranks of the Indian 'Braves', as cannon fodder for the first, vicious charge of the day from the enemy cavalry.

I was seated at the second pair of desks in column one. There were only two naughtier or thicker children between me and the lovely Miss Munn. No matter how badly I behaved or how thick I acted, these two were always thicker and naughtier and I never got any closer to her. I had to settle for third place (not something that sat well with me).

They were the same two kids that I hadn't hit. One was the big, daft lad that I had decided not to tangle with, despite him coming between me and the delectable Miss Munn. The other was a scruffy, scrawny little individual.

To say that he was a bit on the slow side would be something of an understatement. Even Miss Munn, that paragon of patience, used to lose her temper with him and shake him like a rag doll to wake him up. Before long she gave up waiting to lose her temper and just gave him his shaking first thing in the morning come rain or shine.

"I'm just winding him up for the day," she would laugh, as his teeth and knees rattled under the assault, and the whole class laughed with her – except for me. I thought it was disgraceful.

"Teacher's pet," I spat under my breath.

They also used to laugh whenever he wet himself, which was quite often. Miss Munn would make him change into a pair of huge, baggy shorts which she kept especially for this eventuality. Again I was jealous. Making my classmates laugh and getting into Miss Munn's shorts at the same time? It was my idea of heaven.

She was a very physical young lady and, when she was not shaking poor, little Baggy Pants, she spent most of her time lashing out at anyone within range. She had a special treat for the four of us in the danger desks immediately in front of her. Nearly every day we'd be paraded in front of the class and told to hold out our hands. She would then whack them with two wooden rulers held back to back. This brilliant little innovation of hers made a very loud and scary noise and terrified the onlookers, as was intended. Its drawback was that it wasn't as painful as it sounded so it added to the prestige of its regular victims as we stood there nonchalantly and took our punishment with a smirk, under the admiring gaze of the uninitiated.

Meanwhile, Dad had burst an eardrum. He went to hospital to have a plastic one put in. I thought that was great. The bionic man. Soon after this, we had a hearing test at school. The nice lady who had come to test our ears, put a set of earphones on me. "Tell me when you can hear a bleep, John," she said, switching on the machine.

"Bleep," went the machine.

I said nothing.

"Bleeep." A bit louder.

I maintained my silence.

"Bleeeep."

I could tell she was becoming concerned.

"BLEEEEP."

I didn't flinch.

"BLEEEEEEEP...BLAARP...BLEEEEEEEEEP!!!"

She noticed my head twitch slightly as the noise battered my eardrums. "You heard something then, didn't you?"

"Pardon?" I said. By now I was having genuine difficulty hearing.

"BLEEEEEEEEEEEEEEEEEEEEEEEEEEEP!"

The pain was becoming too much so I finally admitted to hearing a faint bleeping noise.

My parents were called into the school to discuss the fact that their son was stone deaf.

"There's nothing wrong with that boy's hearing," snapped Miss Munn, who knew me better than most. "I don't know what his game is, but there is nothing wrong with his hearing."

After much discussion about deaf children's ability to lip-read and cover up their handicap, she was over-ruled and a hospital appointment made to do more extensive tests on my hearing.

When the big day came, my parents took me to the hospital. I thought I was there for an operation and I was a little apprehensive. As we walked down a labyrinth of antiseptic corridors, I became more and more frightened. When at last we reached the doctor, who attempted to usher me into a green-curtained cubicle, I broke down and admitted that I could hear perfectly well.

An explanation was angrily demanded and I blurted out, "I wanted a plastic eardrum like my Dad's."

'Miss Munn, is a bun,' I wrote on the blackboard in retaliation for her crowing that she'd been right all along about my hearing. She was impressed with my grasp of the basic fundamentals of rhyming poetry, and I was impressed with the energetic way in which she wielded her wooden ruler.

"Get out of my sight," she thundered when her whacking arm began to tire.

An old memory stirred at the back of my mind. 'Dare I risk that old ploy?'

I dared.

I shot out of the door, took a sharp left into the boys' cloakroom, then hung upside down by my legs from the coat rail. Miss Munn stormed out of the classroom after me, but she was not quick enough. By the time she passed the cloakroom, I had draped a coat over me and, with nothing dangling, was difficult to detect.

72

When the coast was clear, I lowered myself back to the floor and considered my next move. It would be dangerous to hang around in the cloakroom all day. Even if the teachers didn't catch me, I didn't want to be there when Basher O'Brien came in at lunchtime to pinch the dinner money from our coats. My decision made, I slipped out of school and made my way home.

On the way, a huge Irish Wolfhound jumped up on me and put its paws on my shoulders, knocking me flat on my back. It kept me pinned there for a good five minutes while it licked my face affectionately. I eventually arrived back home, with a very clean face, two hours earlier than expected. Mum immediately became suspicious – I never arrived home with a clean face. She marched me straight back to school where they were organising a search party.

Miss Munn sagged in visible relief when we appeared. "I told him to get out of my sight," she explained to Mum. "I know I shouldn't have said it. Not to *that* boy. I realised it was a mistake as soon as I said it, but it was too late. He was out that door like greased lightning."

She was so relieved at my reappearance that I escaped a beating, so I added this to my repertoire: yell, cry, punch, make others blame themselves for your misdemeanours, misquote them and, if you worry someone enough to make them want to punish you, then worry them some more until your reappearance (or whatever) is greeted with relief rather than anger. These then were my tools for getting my own way whilst avoiding a thrashing, though of course you can't avoid them all.

The most important lesson I'd learnt in punishment

avoidance was still, of course, not to mention that my father's middle name was Humbert. This last point should be strictly adhered to by children with unfortunately named parents and by career-minded persons who do not wish to be passed over for promotion in favour of more subtle colleagues who do not burst into fits of giggles every time their boss's silly name is mentioned.

This even applies in what, on the surface, would appear to be the main exception to the rule – the election of the Pope. In this case, although your fellow cardinals would be delighted if you mentioned their middle names, if you did so then you would be ruining your own chance of election because the man with the silliest name is invariably selected. The best strategy is to shout out your own middle name before collapsing and rolling about in the aisles whilst emitting the most contagious giggles and guffaws you can manage.

Unfortunately, most cardinals are worldly men and so are wise to this age-old ploy. If they can resist the initial urge to snigger, and refuse to be caught up in any Mass hysteria affecting their less experienced brethren, then their chances of election won't go up in a puff of black smoke.

As no sensible cardinal will ever reveal another's daft middle name, and individuals' claims have not always been as silly as the others were led to believe, for the last thousand years or so the popes have in fact invented their own silly names. The first pope guilty of this was Innocent. The others took heart from that and continued the practice.

But enough about that. Let's get back to me. Now that I had developed the social and linguistic skills necessary to allow me to order ice-cream, occasionally get my own way, avoid the odd beating, and spread chaos and confusion at will, I was free to concentrate on money-making ideas. The concept of money as a means of facilitating the exchange of goods, had only recently come to my attention. Before that I had used basic forms of barter such as, "Hand over your sweets or I'll bash you!" This all changed when Dad bought me a piggy bank and I became painfully aware that I had nothing to put in it.

I managed to persuade Dad to give me pocket money, payable in old pennies as their large size and small worth would enable me to fill my beloved piggy bank more quickly. My only financial ambition at this time was to fill my piggy bank to the brim. Every weekend I would empty out my pennies, count them, then lovingly replace them in my grateful piggy, who doffed his little blue hat respectfully on receipt of each coin.

My first financial setback came a short while later. Something in a shop window caught my eye, and I asked Dad to buy it for me.

"You get pocket money now," he told me, "so, if you want something, you have to save up and buy it yourself."

This totally unexpected turn of events was a devastating blow to my first five-year plan to fill my piggy bank. To make matters worse, Harold, who didn't get pocket money, rubbed salt in my wounds by getting Dad to buy him something from the self-same shop. I vowed to give Harold a few wounds of his own at the earliest opportunity, and even spent some of my hard-saved pocket money to buy some salt for the occasion.

How was I supposed to fill my piggy bank when I had to constantly take money out to buy goodies? I realised that I would have to increase my income by something in the order of three hundred percent if I was to keep myself in the manner to which I was accustomed and still fill my piggy bank at the planned rate. I decided to sit at my desk, all day long if necessary, until I had come up with some solution. This led to my second problem. I didn't have a desk. So I made a diversion to the toilet and sat there awaiting inspiration.

The difference between my success and that of Howard Hughes, might be explained by the fact that he was not constantly interrupted by three brothers, two parents, his grandfather, Auntie Betty, and the delivery boy, all constantly banging on the door and demanding to know when he'd be finished as they needed to unload.

"Success is ten percent inspiration and ninety present constipation," I'd shout angrily at each interruption.

It was no good. My thunderous ideas turned out to be mainly wind, with the odd rabbit-dropping of a thought that barely caused a ripple in the S-bend of life. Never-the-less, I decided to put some of these ideas into practice.

My first plan came from a sign I had seen outside a factory on the Lisburn Road. 'FEATHERS BOUGHT – GOOD PRICES PAID,' it stated in bold capitals. This had to be a nice little earner. I enlisted Harold's help and we spent the next week plucking loose feathers from our pillows and eiderdowns, and collecting them in two empty paper gobstopper bags. At the end of this frantic period of clandestine, nocturnal activity, we arrived at the doorstep of the rag-flock factory with our two sweetie bags of plucked feathers in our sweaty little mitts. In the process of knocking on the door, a gust of wind blew one feather away, despite a desperate leap from Harold.

"Drat," I said (strong language indeed), "There goes a fortune."

The door creaked open.

"We've come to sell you some feathers," I proclaimed, as we proudly held out our meagre offerings to the surly-faced individual who appeared.

"Clear off before I give ye's a good skelping," he snarled, swinging a boot in our general direction.

We dropped our feathers and fled empty-handed.

'No more door-to-door selling for me,' I decided. In future I would work from the safety of my own home. I promoted Harold to Chief Salesman, just in case some dangerous outside work became necessary. He didn't read the small print and was delighted with his promotion.

Another idea soon came to me. I had often watched in fascination from the bedroom of Granny W's house, as the drunks staggered up the Shankill Road on a Saturday night, singing and shouting. Granny explained that it was all due to the demon drink. I liked the sound of that. There had to be money in it somewhere.

Grampa W's brother had once run away with the circus when he was fourteen. On the first day of his adventure, as the circus pulled out of town, an old hand shared some over-proof poteen with him. The name, 'poitín' in Irish, derives either from the word 'pota' meaning 'pot' (traditionally it is distilled in a small, pot still), or possibly from 'poit', the Irish word for a hangover. In any case, he woke up to find himself alone at the side of the road, with his head spinning and the circus long gone. He was home in time for tea.

He told me that poteen was made from fermenting potatoes, and that it was very strong. The next day I set about installing a still in my bedroom.

Mum's potatoes mysteriously started to disappear from the pantry in ones or twos. They fired the delivery boy in Grampa M's green grocers shop beneath the flat, but the potatoes kept disappearing. We'd liked the delivery boy because he would sometimes give us a ride in the basket on the front of his bicycle. When we asked what had happened to him, Grampa said that he'd sacked him. We were shocked. We didn't know what it meant but had visions of Grampa beating the poor lad with a sack. We'd have been horrified if he'd said that he'd 'fired' him!

I chopped the missing spuds into little pieces, immersed them in a bowl of water hidden under my bed, and waited for it to turn into poteen.

Mum was becoming suspicious. Not only were her potatoes disappearing at an alarming rate of knots, but a strange odour began to permeate through the flat, though she couldn't tell where it was coming from. We happened to go away on holiday at this time. When we got back home it was no longer difficult to tell where the smell was coming from. Our bedroom had become the first 'No-go' area in Belfast.

This was in the days before the army had developed robots that could be used in controlled explosions, so Mum had to dig out her old Second World War gas mask, tie a rope around her waist, and crawl under my bed to confront whatever it was that lay in wait there. Dad bravely remained at the door, a damp hankie clamped to his nose and mouth, holding the other end of the rope, ready to pull her to safety if she passed out.

She discovered my still and forced a confession from me as to the purpose of the operation. I pleaded innocence as I hadn't realised that distilling poteen was illegal. Dad, whilst not objecting to my project in principle, explained that my methods were all wrong and would not work. He promised to show me how it should be done when I was a little older.

My brothers became caught up in my enthusiasm for making money and decided to go trick-or-treating, it being Halloween. Now this was strictly banned by Dad who regarded the Kray twins as over-grown trick-or-treaters and thought of it as demanding money with menaces. Knowing how strongly he felt about it, for once in my life I decided to take the sensible option and didn't accompany my brothers on their nocturnal rampage.

When Dad caught them (my brothers, not the Krays) they had already made a tidy sum from their enterprise and so didn't object too strongly to the caning they received. It was before the law had been passed allowing the seizure of criminals' assets, so they were allowed to keep their ill-gotten gains to put towards buying fireworks.

I was on the end of the worst beating. Dad would not

believe that I hadn't been with the others and, naturally enough, assumed that I was the ring-leader. He decided to cane me as well. Normally I would say, 'fair cop, governor,' and take my beating lying down, happily letting him whack away to his heart's content. However, I was innocent and could not accept that I was to be caned for something I hadn't done. Every time he tried to take a swing at my bum, I brought my legs up behind me to stop him, while I tried to explain the situation. He kept swinging away at my legs and shouting at me to put them down.

I can't remember which tired first, my legs or his arm, but when he finally stopped, he had the bright idea of asking my brothers if I'd been with them. Harold just smirked at me, but Jock had the decency to confirm that I'd stayed home. Dad offered me an apology, and a penny in compensation. I grudgingly accepted this out-of-court settlement, but for me it was too little too late. I had lost my faith in the judicial system and never regained it. It is too easy for the authorities to make a mistake. That's the reason I don't believe in capital punishment, though, to be fair to Dad, he never made an attempt on my life. No serious attempt anyway.

Dad rarely doubted my word after this. Honesty was about the only virtue I had. A procession of angry parents were sent packing from our door with a flea in their ear after bringing their little Billy's round to complain about me.

Dad would call me to the door. "Did you hit him, John?" he'd ask.

"Yes," I invariably replied, and the mothers would nod indignantly and wait for me to receive my comeuppance.

"Why?" he'd ask.

"Because he called me a f***ing, bast*rd w**ker, Dad," I'd reply sweetly.

Dad would bid them good day and we'd watch, giggling, as little Billy was dragged back down the path with his mother whacking him around the ears for his foul language or other equally reprehensible behaviour as revealed by my good self.

I was always truthful and was certainly not always blameless, but Dad hated precious, uppity kids and felt that, if the parent was uppity enough to complain about me in the first place, then their kid must be a brat and deserved any hiding I had given him. He even secretly made use of me when he did not want to risk losing someone's friendship by personally savaging their unbearable child. A nudge and a nod in the direction of the offending kid was all I needed from Dad. The rest was implicitly understood.

On the subject of unbearable children, Little Harold had now reached that unbearable age. You know the one – the age when they have learnt to speak. This stage tends to last until they have children of their own, and so have no energy left to speak, let alone be unbearable.

Little Harold, to be fair, was more bearable than most unbearable children, but he was still unbearable. The most unbearable thing about him was that he bruised so easily - one tap and he looked as though he'd gone ten rounds with Henry Cooper. This inevitably led us to being subjected to ten rounds with Mum who was desperate to protect her last born, and therefore currently most beloved, offspring. The most beloved, that is, with the exception of her firstborn who, even at this tender age, was given far larger portions at mealtimes than our father ever laid eyes on, never mind cutlery. This led to frequent temper tantrums from Dad, and also to Jock growing taller than him though, at six feet two, our father was not exactly vertically challenged.

Little Harold even found *himself* unbearable because of his vivid imagination and his stubbornness. His problem with stubbornness manifested itself whenever we hit him. He was too much younger than the rest of us (three years below Harold) to put up much physical resistance, so he developed a peculiar form of defence which was ultimately self-defeating. If we smacked him then, instead of looking suitably chastised, he would burst out laughing. Of course this meant that we would hit him again, but a bit harder. The harder we smacked him, the harder he laughed. The harder he laughed, the angrier we'd get and the harder we'd hit him. This vicious circle, and it often became vicious, would continue until his sides were so sore from laughing that he'd burst into tears. For the sake of his pride then, every time he committed a minor misdemeanour for which he would receive a gentle, brotherly cuff to keep him in line, he always ended up being beaten black and blue (not difficult given his propensity for bruising).

He did have the occasional victory with this technique. Sometimes he would still be laughing when we decided that it would be imprudent to dish out any more punishment, and we'd have to angrily stalk away leaving him battered and bruised, but still in possession of the battlefield and having the last laugh. If he ever ends up in court for a speeding offence he'll be dragged down to the cells to begin his two-year sentence for contempt of court thinking, 'That showed him!'

Little Harold's imagination also helped to make his own life unbearable – with a little bit of help from his brothers. He was very susceptible to suggestion. During our frequent all-in wrestling bouts, if Little Harold was at the bottom of the pile (which was often the case) we'd whisper in his ear, "Little Harold, you can't breathe."

"CAN'T BREATHE, CAN'T BREATHE, CAN'T BREATHE," he'd yell at the top of his voice, thus proving that he could. Total panic would eventually set in and he would struggle uncontrollably until we let him up, then he'd run to the nearest window for air.

It was whilst leaning out the window, gulping in unnecessarily large quantities of air, that Little Harold's obsession with hats reached a new level. There was a man walking down the Lisburn Road with a little boy who was wearing a blue and white bobble hat similar to one greatly loved titfer recently lost by Little Harold.

Jock scented a chance for mischief. "Look, Little Harold," he said, pointing out the innocent young lad. "That boy's got your hat!"

Little Harold was down the stairs and out into the busy main road as fast as his three-year-old legs could carry him.

Realising what he'd done, Jock set off in pursuit with Harold and I close behind. Little Harold reached his prey before we could catch up with him. He was jumping up and down, trying to whip the hat from the startled boy's head, while his father was holding the hat in place with one hand and swiping at Little Harold with the other.

"Fek off you mad little bugger," he yelled between swipes.

"That's my hat," Little Harold screamed back, still jumping up and down and swinging from the hat whenever he managed to get a hand hold.

We dragged him away, still hurling insults after the fast-retreating pair and insisting it was *his* hat. When we eventually got him home and forced him through the door and back up the stairs to the flat, he angrily ran off to tell Mum and Dad. He was livid when they took the side of the hat thieves.

Smarting from this injustice, and from the smack on the bum he got for running out to the busy main street, he decided to run away from home. Having rolled up a couple of biscuits, a clean pair of socks and a gob-stopper in a handkerchief, and tied it to the end of a stick (Little Harold has always carefully planned his mad, impetuous moments) he stuck Harold's hat on his head and made his way to the nearest bus stop.

A bus arrived at about the same moment that Mum realised he was missing. With that sixth sense peculiar to mothers, she glanced out of the window and spotted him as he climbed aboard. Skirts flying, she gave chase.

"And what are you doing out on your own, Sunny Jim?" the conductor asked as Little Harold bustled past him.

"My name's, Little Harold," Sunny Jim replied indignantly.

The conductor held the bus up as he quizzed the runaway. "And where are you going, Little Harold?"

"To my Granny's."

"And where might that be, young man?" he asked patiently. "An address would be helpful."

"MY GRANNY'S HOUSE!" Little Harold shouted. The man was obviously an imbecile.

"Do you have the bus fare by any chance?"

Little Harold reluctantly handed over his gobstopper, but not before giving it a crafty lick.

At this moment, Mum arrived at full belt and dragged the disgruntled midget from the bus. He kicked and screamed as the bus pulled away. The conductor still had his gobstopper.

He learned an important lesson that day. Never part with your gobstopper until you'd got what you want. This philosophy tended to bring him more sorrow than joy over the years, but he persisted with it and, as far as I'm aware, is persisting with it still.

Little Harold's obsession with hats also caused him to fall out with his favourite Auntie. Most weekends we'd stay with our Mum's parents on the Shankill Road. Uncle Hugh and Auntie May lived just around the corner, and my brothers and I would pay them a visit on Saturday afternoons. Auntie May had no children off her own and always spoilt us rotten, so we always looked forward to our visits.

Uncle Hugh worked at the Ulster Museum in Stranmillis, and he enjoyed scaring us with stories of the Egyptian mummy coming to life in the dead of night. We all enjoyed the tall tales, with the exception of Little Harold who grassed him up to Granny. Uncle Hugh was promptly banned from telling us scary stories but, one dark and gloomy afternoon, he could resist no longer and gave in to my pleading. Having bottled up his tales for some time, he unleashed a particularly hair-raising one that even had *me*, a big boy of seven, quaking in my boots.

Little Harold was terrified and angry with Uncle Hugh for scaring him, so he decided to retaliate. "You're not Uncle Hugh," he shouted, "you're UNCLE CANOE!"

We were horrified but Little Harold was not yet satisfied. Uncle Hugh did not look suitably chastised by the 'canoe' jibe, and even had what looked suspiciously like a grin quivering at the corner of his mouth. So Little Harold struck again.

"You're…you're…you're, UNCLE POO!" he yelled.

We'd heard enough. Our visions of future Saturday afternoon marshmallow treats were shrivelling up and disappearing before our eyes. Apologising profusely, we dragged Little Harold out into the street, but he wasn't finished yet. Uncle Hugh, who for some reason didn't seem as mortified as us by this attack on his dignity by a three-year-old, had followed us outside, with Auntie May in tow.

Little Harold spun around and stared at them. "Where's my hat?" he demanded to know.

'Oh, Good Father,' we thought. There'd be no stopping him now.

"You didn't bring a hat with you, Little Harold," Auntie May told him sweetly.

"I had a hat," he insisted. "Where is it?"

"You weren't wearing a hat when you arrived, Little Harold." Auntie May was struggling to maintain her sweet smile, unlike Uncle Hugh who was grinning from ear to ear and loving every minute of it.

"I was. I had a hat. YOU'VE GOT MY HAT!"

Auntie May shook her head and shrugged apologetically at the neighbours who'd come out to enjoy the commotion.

"SHE'S GOT MY HAT!" Little Harold yelled down the street as he pointed straight at her. Auntie May looked mortified, but the accusing finger never wavered. "SHE'S GOT MAY HAT. SHE'S GOT MY HAT!"

Horrified, I managed to avoid Little Harold's gnashing teeth, and clamped my hand firmly over his mouth to stop the tirade. Jock and Harold grabbed his arms and we dragged him, kicking and bucking, across the street.

When we reached the other side he broke free just long enough to shout across at our embarrassed auntie, "THIEF! I HAD A HAT!"

Furious in the certainty that we'd never again be allowed to visit Auntie May, we boy-handled Little Harold back to Granny's house where we told everyone all the gory details of his disgraceful behaviour. We waited indignantly for him to receive his just deserts, but instead they all burst out laughing.

Adults. I'll never understand them.

For some reason we were not banned from our visits. Most Saturdays, when we arrived back from Auntie May's, stuffed to the gunnels with goodies, Granny, not to be outdone by her little sister, put out plates of buns and biscuits for us.

"Which bun would you like, Grampa," I would always politely ask before helping myself. When he pointed one out I would grab it and gobble it up, choking on cake and chortles. This process would be repeated by each of my brothers until only one sorry-looking bun was left, surrounded by the crumbs and other detritus that we'd coughed up during our cake-filled cackles. Grampa would smile on benignly.

Dad's dad, Grampa M, a stern Presbyterian, was a different kettle of fish to Grampa W. One evening, out of character, he had actually put out cakes and buns. Confident of the rules of the game, before getting stuck in I asked, "Which one would you like, Grampa?"

"Good boy." He nodded approval at my etiquette as he held out his plate. "I'll have the one with the cherry."

Chortling, I snaffled it up.

The slap he gave me nearly knocked me off my chair.

Adults. I'll never understand them.

Our two grandfathers were chalk and cheese. In contrast to the stern Grampa M, Grampa W loved a tipple; was very fond of spending his money as quickly as he earned it; and was demonstratively fond of his grandchildren – well, any children for that matter. He would combine these three loves on a Friday evening when he had just been paid. His first stop, if he managed to evade Granny at the shipyard gates, was the pub in the company of his workmates. After a few whiskeys, in a jolly mood, he would meander up the Shankill Road towards home. Knowing his generosity when under the influence, gangs of local kids would follow him up the street. He'd throw handfuls of coins in the air and watch tenderly as the little angels tore each other to shreds to get at the money. He would then stroll on, happily oblivious to the bloody carnage behind him.

He'd do the same with us when we were visiting, throwing his change in the air and shouting, "Scramble." Then we'd battle it out for a share of the coins. Generally speaking, the profits went in age order as survival of the fittest took its brutal course.

One afternoon he'd been in the pub at lunchtime and came home to find us visiting. He had no change left, having been particularly generous with the local scallywags on his way home – due to the landlord being particularly generous with his measures earlier. Seeing our eager little faces, he could not find it in his heart to deny us, even though he could not find it in his pockets to pay us. So he emptied his pay packet and threw the notes in the air.

"SCRAM...AAAUGH!" he yelled.

Granny was on him before he could finish his cry, scattering her grandchildren left and right as she pounced on her endangered house-keeping money.

Little Harold was Grampa's favourite. This was because he was the youngest and most gullible of us, and therefore the easiest target for Grampa's tall tales. He would sit Little Harold down on his knee and say, "Do you remember the time the Red Indians had me tied to a totem pole, and you rescued me?"

"Yes, Grampa, I remember," said Little Harold, gazing up at him and taking in every word as the story unfolded.

"You crept right through them as they were dancing around the fire, getting ready to roast me."

"Yes I did, Grampa. I did."

Little Harold believed every word of every tall tale and really thought that he'd been there (wherever 'there' happened to be).

"And you cut through the ropes with a knife and got me free, didn't you?"

"Yes, Grampa."

"Weren't you scared?"

"Not at all."

"Then one of them spotted us, but you plucked a feather from an ostrich, stuck it in your hair, and spoke to him in Apache, and he let us pass. What was it you said to him?"

"How?" ventured Little Harold.

"Your exact words," said Grampa. "And what was the name of the horse we got away on?"

"Uhmmmm…"

"You remember the one. It was a beautiful, big black stallion. What was its name again?"

"Uhmmmm…Goldie?"

"That's the one," grinned Grampa.

"Yes, I remember now," said Little Harold, reassured that he had really been there. "It was Goldie."

When we returned home to the Lisburn Road at the end of the weekend, we'd climb the stairs to the first floor, above the shop; climb some more stairs to get to the bathroom to empty our bowels and bursting bladders; climb back down again as the bathroom was a blind alley; climb another set of stairs to our bedroom; remember that we'd forgotten to brush our teeth and so climb back down and up and down, and back up again, before finally falling, exhausted, into bed.

Being children, as soon as our sleepy heads touched the pillow, we were wide awake again. To pass the interminable minutes between going to bed and drifting off to sleep, we made up several games. One of these 'very interesting' games was 'Cops and robbers'. The headlights of passing cars chased each other across the bedroom ceiling. We decided that the bright ones were the robbers, and the dull ones were the cops in hot pursuit. It was stimulating stuff. Mum and Dad liked that game as we were usually fast asleep in a matter of seconds.

Another game was the fantastic adventures of Freddy Fox, Teddy and Ted. Ted was so named because, as Harold's elder brother, I had first call on the name of my toy bear and went for the imaginative moniker of, Teddy. Deprived of this, his preferred option but one that I would not tolerate, Harold racked his brains and came up with the even more imaginative, Ted. I was a bit disgruntled as it was too close to Teddy for comfort, but decided to let him off with it.

Yet another game was the exploits of our imaginary horses, Thunder, Lightning, and Sam.

SAM!!!

As far as Jock and I were concerned, this wasn't on. It took away from the dynamics of the stories we made up as we flashed across the skies on Thunder and Lightning, and then Harold would plod up on Sam. We tempted him with exciting names like Champion, Sky-Rider, or Cloud Leaper, but he was adamant and, despite constant beatings, pleadings and cajolings, his horse remained Sam. It infuriated Jock and me, and it is only now that I can sit back and quietly admire his choice and his obstinacy. Thunder, Lightning and Sam – it does have a certain ring to it.

Harold and I also invented two characters called Stupid, and Sergeant Shut-up. We played this night after night. Stupid would say something stupid, and Sergeant Shut-up would say, "Shut up, Stupid!" It entertained us for years.

A decade later, 'It Ain't Half Hot Mum' hit the screens, but we had no proof that we'd invented the main characters back in 1964, so we couldn't sue for royalties.

CHAPTER 5

ONWARD TO VICTORY

I'm going to take a break for some holidays now. While we were based in Germany, we'd been on holidays in Holland, Switzerland, Austria, Luxembourg and Liechtenstein, which was pretty privileged for that time I guess, as few people travelled abroad. Unfortunately, I was too young to remember any of them. My first holiday memories are of more exotic places such as Bangor, Port Rush, and Donegal.

In Donegal we pitched our tent in the garden of an old, derelict house on the wild and largely deserted Atlantic coast. We were forbidden to enter the house because a giant billy-goat lived there. At least that's what Dad told us. I'm beginning to have my doubts now. Perhaps we would have been more in danger of the roof falling in than being attacked by a huge, troll-eating billy-goat, but I know which warning was the more effective with four young boys. Come to think of it, Dad emerged from several forays into the cottage, with barely a bite-mark on him.

The first holiday that really sticks in my mind is the one

that we spent at 'The Little Red Cottage', on Carlingford Lough, near Warrenpoint in County Down. Uncle John and Auntie Dorothy, with our two young cousins, Carolyn and Julia, along with our Grandparents and various other friends and relatives who came and went on a daily basis, crowded into this tiny little cottage, along with our branch of the clan. It must have been 1966, because the men snuck off to the pub to watch the England vs West Germany World Cup Final.

It was here that I met the first big love of my life - the delectable Sylvia. Even as holiday romances go, it did not last long – about two hours in fact. This was because she kept wanting to kiss me and, after a first, tentative, experimental peck, I decided that I wanted nothing more to do with it.

"Typical man," she snapped. "Once they've got what they wanted, they dump you!"

I had only put up with her in the first place because Jock was having a steamy affair with an older woman. She must have been nearly ten years old. Jock's girl was a beautiful, statuesque creature with deep, sea-blue eyes and a mane of long, blonde, sun-kissed hair. Mine was a scrawny red-head with a rash of freckles. My brothers teased me for years about her tangled mess of red hair, freckles, ugly face and glasses. It infuriated me because she hadn't worn glasses.

A couple of years ago I found an old photograph that Dad had taken of Sylvia at the time. There she was in all her glory - freckles, mop of red hair, ugly face but – no glasses. I travelled the length and breadth of the country, visiting my brothers and triumphantly waving the picture in their startled faces. "See!" I'd shout. "NO GLASSES!" Unfortunately they did not even remember Sylvia, let alone whether or not she had worn glasses, so it took a bit of the sheen off my victory. However, I have a long memory when I feel I have been unfairly slighted, and I felt that justice had been done. At last I could lay the ghost of Sylvia to rest and move on with my life.

This holiday was also the first time we met our cousins who lived in London. Mum's sister had married a half French, quarter Italian, quarter Romanian man. This made their daughters (apart from confused) half Irish, quarter French, eighth Italian, eighth Romanian, English girls. "I say old chap, dobre den mon amis, arriverderci, to be sure," was Carolyn's first sentence.

Uncle Jacques never quite caught on to the Irish sense of humour. Once, when he was putting up Christmas decorations, he dropped a drawing pin, tried to catch it, overbalanced, and fell off the stepladder he'd been standing on. He landed arse-first on the drawing pin he'd just dropped. As he hopped about, cursing and clutching his punctured derriere, he couldn't understand why his loving wife was howling with laughter. Another time, he was hauling a wardrobe upstairs. He had the door open to give himself a better grip. He'd nearly reached the top when he slipped and fell into the wardrobe. The door slammed shut on him as the wardrobe hurtled down the stairs. Dazed and bruised, he tentatively pushed the wardrobe door open, only to be greeted by the sight of his loving wife with tears of laughter streaming down her face.

Once again, he didn't see the funny side and was deeply hurt by her reaction.

Cousin Julia was only a baby, but Carolyn was a mature young woman of one years old. She walked and talked fluently, (Is it possible to walk fluently? I suppose it is if you cut down on your alcohol intake), and she held forth on such topics as the Cuban Missile Crisis, the abolition of the death penalty, and the origins of man.

She was infuriatingly stubborn in her beliefs, and it took all our powers of persuasion to make her understand when she was mistaken. For example, she refused to accept that babies are found under gooseberry bushes and had nothing to do with the hare-brained, and frankly quite disgusting, theory that she had in her tiny head. Her parents believed in telling children the truth whereas our Mum and Dad believed in lying through their teeth – which was much more fun. What's Christmas to a child, without Santa Claus?

Carolyn was allowed to stay up debating affairs of state with the adults, long after we'd been sent to bed. This, of course, infuriated us. To make matters worse, she would come over and chat to us while we were being tucked up in bed for the night. Actually, that is not strictly true. Young Carolyn did not chat. She pontificated, debated, or held forth on any subject you cared to name, but she did not indulge in idle chit-chat. We resented these late-night visits as we big men of the world were in bed while this young whipper-snapper was allowed to stay up. On top of this we did not regard 'The Life of Samuel Johnson' by James Boswell, as suitable material and we demanded that, if she insisted on reading us a bed-time story, it should be 'Sleeping Beauty' or 'Snow White and the Seven Dwarfs'.

Despite these faults, we all thought Carolyn was adorable; all of us except Little Harold that is. He was used to being the youngest and therefore most fussed-over member of the family. The presence of Carolyn and baby Julia, put his nose out of joint – and he has a big nose.

One morning as the sun was slowly rising over the horizon, its golden fingers glistening off the tranquil waters of Carlingford Lough, Little Harold stole silently from the cottage while everyone else still slept. In one hand he held his toy spade, and in the other, one of Carolyn's shoes. With ninja-like stealth, he emerged from the shadows of the porch and made his way noiselessly across the garden, pausing and sniffing the wind for danger as he reached the flowerbed. Nothing stirred. Satisfied that the coast was clear, he set about his wicked work. The spade was a blur of movement as the earth parted beneath his maddened onslaught, then the shoe was deposited in the hole and quickly covered with dirt again. Within seconds there was no sign that he had ever been there as he retreated like a wraith, back the way he had come.

Later in the morning, when Mum came to wake us, Little Harold was tucked up in bed sleeping the sleep of the unjust, the happy dream he was obviously having, etched into the corners of his mouth. He looked so content that Mum let him lie in. This uniquely 'Little Harold' protest was the only sign he ever gave that something was amiss in his relationship with his cousin.

Little Harold had a thing about shoes. He went straight

97

from an obsession with hats, to one about shoes, missing out all the bits in between – which was probably just as well. Once he came home from the park, with no shoes on. Minutes later our next-door neighbour stormed in with her equally shoeless daughter in tow. Little Harold, it transpired, had sailed one of his shoes out onto the large pond in the park, to see if it would float. It did. It floated out of reach into the middle of the pond. He then launched his second shoe to bring back the first, but this one also became becalmed, just out of reach.

Never one to give up on a totally useless plan just because it did not, and never would, work, Little Harold then relieved his young companion of her shoes and sent them out on the same mission with the same disastrous result. Dumbfounded at the lack of success of his carefully thought-out rescue plan, he then pulled her socks off and threw them at the slowly sinking shoes. Still no success. In desperation he hurled in his own socks and then, having run out of footwear and with no plan B, he had to admit defeat and limped home. A confession having been wrung from him, Dad then wore out a perfectly good pair of slippers on Little Harold's bony bum.

Within twenty minutes of launching his summer offensive, two pairs of shoes were dead, two pairs of socks missing in action, and one pair of slippers would never work again; not to mention a young boy's wounded pride and glowing-red buttocks. Like General Haig before him, Little Harold insisted that his plan would have worked if he'd had sufficient supplies of ammunition. Unlike the Government of the time, Dad did not accept this explanation and refused to tighten up drinking laws to ensure that no shoe-production was lost through drunkenness. Also, unlike General Haig, Little Harold was sent to bed with no supper.

Meanwhile, Jock made the horrifying discovery that his 'holiday' girlfriend lived two streets away from us in Belfast. It was a bit too close for comfort. He didn't want his friends finding out that he'd kissed a girl. He dropped her like the hot potato she undoubtedly was. It broke her heart and she didn't get over it for minutes, but Jock didn't care. He always was a cad.

It had been a long, hot glorious summer and hay bales were piled in the fields. Having been city boys for a while now, we loved this time in the country. My brothers and I, used the hay bales to build a daddy-proof fortress. The daddy-proofing consisted of making only a small, child-sized entrance to our den. This was necessary because Dad had banned us from playing in haystacks upon pain of pain. This, he told us, was because one of us, or one of our friends, would probably be stupid enough to play with matches, and we could all burn to death. He turned out to be right. One of our friends *was* stupid enough to light a match in our highly inflammable fort. He was wrong about us burning to death though, but we couldn't gloat publicly without giving ourselves away.

Dad did find us though. Foolishly, we allowed ourselves to be late for tea one evening, and he came looking for us. Ignoring his calls, we kept our silence as we hid behind the walls of our straw castle, secure in the knowledge that he couldn't fit through the kid-sized gateway. Unfortunately for us, being a military man, he was up to the challenge. Always one for direct action, he discounted the idea of laying siege and waiting ten minutes for hunger to flush us out. Instead, he huffed and puffed then pulled the walls down and chased us home, squealing like the three little pigs. As we were on holiday, and the fool playing with matches was not one of us, he showed some leniency and we only received a tongue lashing.

It was also on this holiday that I first tried my hand at canoeing. Dad had built a two-man canoe with his own fair hands – and the thing actually floated. He found this out by sticking Mum in the canoe, tying a bit of rope to one end, and pushing her out to sea. He eventually pulled her back in again when her terrified screams (she couldn't swim) started to irritate him. The canoe was still dry, apart from the seat that Mum had been on, so he concluded that the trials had been successful and it was sea-worthy.

Once the canoe had been thoroughly swilled out, Dad plonked me on the front seat, jumped in the back, and paddled off. I let him do all the paddling, not because I'm lazy (although I am) but because he didn't trust me with a paddle. He was afraid that I might be overcome with one of my bursts of enthusiasm and that a sudden burst of rampant paddling might carry us out to sea before he could regain control.

My next chance to go canoeing came many years later when I joined the Bristol Polytechnic Canoe Club. The instructor had the bright idea of teaching us the 'Eskimo Roll' before we'd even learned to paddle. It would give us the confidence to do anything else, he declared. So I spent each week capsizing and then rolling back up the other side – which was to set the pattern for the rest of my life. I became very proficient at this and could roll either way, with or without a paddle. But, as this was all we did week after week, I soon became bored and left the club.

Back home, at the end of term, I borrowed Little Harold's canoe and had all the family impressed with my skills and thinking that I was a champion canoeist. This impression only lasted until Dad called me back in. They soon realised that I had no idea how to paddle or to steer the canoe. All I could do was roll over and over. I came last in the local regatta.

The next holiday we went on upset Little Harold. We were driving in the south of Ireland, when I became curious about where we were going. In answer to my question, Dad flung back over his shoulder, "We're going to Kilkenny."

Little Harold burst into tears.

"It's not that bad," Mum tried to comfort him. (She'd obviously never been before.) "Why are you crying?"

"I don't want to kill Kenny," he sobbed.

Kenny was his best friend.

Another time we went on holiday with some Catholic friends of our parents, and their little girls. Dad hired a cottage in the countryside, with a small brook running across the bottom of the garden. We found out two great secrets at this time. One was the 'echo', which we discovered coming back from a nearby wood. We spent hours shouting at it and listening to the replies. It was a bit like married life, but with listening thrown in.

Our other discovery was even more amazing. We'd always been aware that Catholics were meant to be different from Protestants, but we didn't know why. That night, as we furtively watched the girls getting ready for bed, we finally spotted the difference.

Another early memory I have was of an outing rather than a holiday. We were on a children's day out to the seaside, organised by our church. There had been a plague of jellyfish with hundreds of them washed up on the beach. Both Harold and I had been stung in the past and were terrified of standing on them as Dad had told us they can still sting if you stamp on them. Our fellow day-trippers had no such fears and tramped over them with no apparent harm done (not to the children anyway). Supported by the memory of our stings, we decided to ignore the evidence of our eyes and big brother Jock's demands, and we heeded Dad's advice not to stand on them. This was extremely difficult considering that they covered most of the surface of the beach. We got into contortions trying to avoid them, our progress slowing to crawling pace, and we fell further and further behind the rest of the group.

As the main body of the outing threatened to get out of sight, Jock decided to play the hero and go for help. That's what he told us anyway. As he took off after the other trippers, leaving Harold and I stranded and lost, we formed the opinion that he'd panicked and done a runner, leaving us to our fate. But to be fair to him, he did eventually return with one of the trip supervisors, by which time we had already been rescued from the beach by a kind family and

102

were now being treated to an ice-cream each.

Jock was doubly put out as, once again, he didn't get an ice-cream, and also his heroic efforts in finding help were not appreciated by our parents who told him off for abandoning his little brothers. And serves him right too, we thought. In retrospect though, I feel that Jock was hard done by. It must have been a painfully difficult decision for a seven-year-old to make, leaving his little brothers, to go and seek help. Now I believe that his wading through the jellyfish was an act of bravery rather than cowardice. This came home to me later on a holiday at Findhorn in Scotland. A Portuguese Man-o War, had been washed up on the beach (well a huge, brown jellyfish anyway. We thought it must be a Man-o-War.) A holiday friend of ours decided to jump on it and he was badly stung. Dad had been right after all. The boy's leg swelled up to twice its normal size. He was in agony and was carted off to hospital. It was a miracle that he kept his leg.

Not that Findhorn needed miracles. This was the late sixties and Findhorn was a miracle in its own right. It had made the desert bloom, or at least managed to grow vegetables in the inhospitable environment of sand dunes on the North East coast of Scotland. This was a phenomenon that gained world-wide coverage. While we were there on holiday though, we spent most of our time gathering and making compost and piling it into pits that had been dug out of the sand. All the sand did was to form giant flowerpots for the massive doses of compost where the vegetables were grown – not much of a miracle in my eyes, but who knows?

I had no problem with the labour, but I did with the food. The community was vegetarian and it was nuts for breakfast, dinner and tea. It was all very basic in those days and I hated it. It was meant to be a two-week holiday, but they let us stay for free for an extra fortnight because of our valuable labour. I nearly starved to death and only survived the month by wearing wellies and chewing on my leather shoes.

Most of the adults at the camp were into peace and love, Jesus and flower power. They were a kind and hospitable lot. The same could not be said for the children though. We had made a group of friends and the leader of the gang was a big lad with a nasty disposition. Much against the aspirations of the place, he formed us into an 'army' platoon with himself as the self-appointed sergeant in charge. His favourite 'game' was dishing out corporal punishment to anyone falling foul of his rules (which he made up on the spot).

His favourite whipping boy was a skinny wee lad, a lot younger than him, and he gave him a lot of stick. One day though, he made a mistake. He hit my brother, Harold. I went looking for him and, to the amazement of the others who were terrified of him, I gave him a good hiding. Sadly, I basked in the glory of my triumph for only one day. The big lad tried to regain his reputation and his position by hitting the skinny boy again, but the scrawny young lad had taken heart from my fight – and he gave the bully another thrashing. I was devastated. If the little waif could beat the bully then anybody could. It totally devalued my heroic efforts and I was thoroughly miffed.

However, the bully kept a low profile after that, and the life of us kids became a lot more peaceful and pleasant.

An embarrassing moment came when we were on holiday in Wales. We were visiting St. David's Cathedral and were in a small chapel at the back, shut off from the main cathedral by some doors. Dad, a keen photographer at the time, saw an opportunity for a good snap. The caption, 'St. John and the Pilgrim', had already sprung into his head. He wanted me in the pulpit, wagging my finger at Harold, who would be sitting in the front pew. The problem was that there were a few other tourists hanging around and Dad didn't want to appear sacrilegious by our crossing the roped-off area and mounting the pulpit, so we waited for them to leave. However, the longer we waited, the more of them appeared.

Dad eventually lost patience and ordered me over the top. I clambered over the rope barrier and made my way doggedly across no-mans-land to the pulpit where I dutifully wagged my finger at Harold, despite my embarrassment in front of the tutting, disapproving, and ever-growing throng in the chapel. Dad, always oblivious to public opinion unless it agreed with his own, ignored them and took his time setting up the photograph. Eventually he was satisfied and I was at last allowed to shuffle out through the glares of the gathered people. When we reached the door the vicar appeared and held it open for us to depart. "You're welcome to join us for evensong," was his parting remark.

They weren't tourists, they were the congregation we

had been holding up for the early evening service. I was highly embarrassed, but Dad was delighted.

On the subject of vicars, when she was little, Mum used to keep the local minister amused. He'd called round for tea one evening, and Granny told Mum to sing him a song. She scandalised everyone by singing, 'Our Eileen's Blue Drawers'. He loved it, and teased strait-laced Aunt Eileen about it whenever he saw her. Mum then told him that he'd never go to heaven because he told lies. He'd said he'd take her for a ride in his car (she'd never been in one) and he hadn't done it. She finished off by telling him that her dad always hid upstairs when he saw him coming.

I think that is enough about holidays for now, except to warn you of some of the dangers of camping with small children (tents are far more reliable.) The first rule is not to pitch your tent on a slope. Secondly, if you must camp on a slope then tie your children to the tent pole before going to sleep. During a camping holiday our parents awoke one morning to find no sign of Jock, though they were fairly sure he had been there the night before. Dad was delighted as he thought, with Jock out of the way, he might at last get decent-sized meal. However, his hopes were dashed when Mum insisted on searching for their firstborn.

They found him pretty easily. He was about ten yards from the tent, still in his sleeping bag and dozing contentedly where he had come to rest after sliding out through the tent flap during the night. He was in the middle of a herd of cows and was very lucky that nothing of a noxious nature had fallen on him from a great height. The cows were lucky as well because, if anything ever happened to Jock, then I always retaliated in kind. I'm not sure how I would have managed it but I'd have found a way.

Dad left the Royal Air Force with a sizeable pension which he withdrew as a lump sum and put in his back pocket. Considering the size of the wad, he could have ended up with a nasty limp if someone had not operated quickly to remove it. Luckily for him there was a quick operator on hand.

Having filled in the time by helping out in Grampa's greengrocery shop, delivering customers' orders to their homes, Dad decided to go into business himself. The sharks licked their lips as he took his first tentative (but not tentative enough) steps into the world of commerce. The owner of a textile firm in Belfast, was looking for someone with lots of money but little business sense, to buy into partnership with him. Dad fitted the bill perfectly. He was not quite as naive as his prospective business partner may have hoped, and he had an accountant take a close look at the company's books. The set that he was shown were in a lot better shape than the ones that remained hidden under the counter, and the accountant advised Dad that it was a good proposition. It was – but not for our father. As soon as the money had changed hands his new-found business partner headed for the border faster than a Saharan ice-cream salesman on mid-summer's day.

With his now ex-partner safely ensconced in the Irish

Republic, Dad was left at the helm of a rapidly sinking ship, and all the debts and liabilities soon made themselves known to him. The highly unseaworthy company went under within a few months, a dock strike in Liverpool putting the final nail in the coffin. The circumstances being what they were (he was the victim of fraudulent accounting) he escaped being declared personally bankrupt, but he was declared well and truly skint.

He tried to claw back some money by selling the remaining stock door to door from a van, a job he hated with a vengeance. Ever the snob, he took us to one side. "Don't ever tell anyone that your father is a ... *draper*!" he warned us in a stern whisper, scared of being overheard.

"We won't, Dad," we solemnly promised as we cowered together under his withering stare. We were as worried as he was that word might get out. We had no idea what a draper was but, from the look on his face and the blood-curdling threats that he issued, we knew that it must be something really terrible – like being called, 'Humbert'!

Dad was not a draper for very long. No one bought anything. They didn't have much chance to. He would knock on a door then run away, terrified that someone might recognise him. You had to be an early bird with wings to match if you wanted to buy anything from our father. Even if the door opened suddenly, before he lost his nerve and made a run for it, he would hide his wares behind his back and deny he was selling anything. Curiosity drove some people to find out what he was up to and, when he refused to show them what he was selling, they had to have it, whatever it was and whatever the price.

These occasional accidental but lucrative deals kept our heads above water for a while, but not for long. Dad was forced to go on the BRU (the dole). Once again we were forbidden from telling anyone. "He's not a draper anymore," I replied defensively to anyone who asked what my father did for a living.

A family of six, we were surviving on six pounds a week Social Security. We were living with Grampa M, so we didn't have to pay rent, which was a blessing (my pocket money wouldn't have stretched that far). Also, with it being a grocers shop, we did not go short of food. Unfortunately, it was a greengrocers and so, after a few weeks, we were all feeling a little green ourselves, and praying that we'd never see another lettuce as long as we lived. We hoped that Dad would find another job soon – preferably at a butcher's shop.

Mum and Dad tried hard to make sure that we did not know how poor we were. For our part we tried to keep from our parents the fact that we knew. We stopped pestering them for toys and sweets, like most children do, and were happy with anything we *did* get.

One major digression from this was when Jock, in an argument about bed-time, announced that he was a big boy now and could stay awake all night. Dad decided to call his bluff and a bet was struck. At stake was an undertaking to go to bed with no arguing, versus a toy gun called a 'Johnny Seven'. This remarkable weapon carried the plastic equivalent of seven of the best means of destruction then known to man – with the exception of plastic explosives.

It cost about six pounds, which was a week's income for the family at that time. I knew how little money our parents had and I was not going to stand for Jock relieving them of what little they had – not without me getting in on the act anyway. I managed to wangle myself into the deal and so stood to pick up a second Johnny Seven for myself if I could stay awake all night as well. Dad cast a worried glance at Harold but he just yawned and fell asleep, much to Dad's relief. Mum was furious at Dad for risking two weeks income but he insisted that we would not be able to stay awake all night, so there was nothing to worry about.

That night, on the hour, every hour, he popped into our bedroom to check if we were asleep yet. "Hi, Dad," we greeted him cheerily, and he stomped out again looking a little bit more worried each time. As the long night wore on, his visits became more and more frequent and frantic. By the last hour before dawn, he was appearing every few minutes and looking far more haggard and tired than we were. Ironically it was only these frenetic visits that kept us awake during that long, last, sleepy hour. Long after the sun had crept over the horizon, Dad finally conceded defeat. We'd won our bet. Happy, but exhausted, we fell asleep at last.

That afternoon, when we finally got up and shook Dad awake, he honoured his word, emptied his bank account, pilfered the house-keeping money, and took us to the shop. Fifteen minutes later we were the proud owners of two Johnny Sevens, and the envy of the local kids.

For the next few months we terrorised the neighbourhood with our guns, and ate an awful lot of lettuce. This was the first time plastic bullets had been used on the streets of Belfast and the howls of the angry shoppers that we were trying to disperse went some way towards drowning out the sound of Mum shouting at Dad non-stop for eight weeks. After two months, to the shoppers' relief, we ran out of bullets – which was hardly surprising, considering our diet.

Our diet improved briefly when Dad borrowed some money and acquired a tipper lorry. He worked the construction sites for a while but the religious divide left him on the fringes and not receiving any decent contracts, the construction industry being a mainly Catholic concern at the time. He soon disposed of the vehicle, at a handsome loss, to the same unsurprised gentleman who'd sold it to him in the first place. We went back to eating lettuce.

His next project was buying old houses with a partner who was a builder (a Catholic as it happened), doing them up, and selling at a profit. This time he had a partner who didn't let him down, in fact Phil and his wife, Lena, became friends for life with Mum and Dad. If they'd been doing this at the right time and in the right place, then they'd have made their fortunes. Unfortunately, Belfast in the mid-sixties was neither the right time nor the right place. Mum had the lettuce washed and ready by the time Dad realised there was no money to be made and reluctantly laid down his paintbrush.

With the 'huge' profits he had made in the property business, Dad bought us all ukuleles. These were only toys with actual string strings and wooden pegs for pretending to tune them. Dad screwed on proper tuning heads and restrung the instruments with cat gut. (He told us they were nylon strings but we noticed there were very few stray cats in the neighbourhood for quite some time.) He thereby turned the toys into working ukuleles but at a quarter of the price. He then taught us how to play them, which was quite impressive as he didn't know how to play one himself. This led to the rather unique and nerve-jarring technique that we all developed.

Our first gig was at the Methodist church we attended on Sundays. They suggested that we became Presbyterians. Undeterred, Dad sent us out to busk, fully equipped and armed with a fine repertoire of two songs, onto the mean streets of Belfast, and he waited for the money to pour in. When, for some strange reason, this did not materialise, he set out once more to try and find gainful employment.

Then our luck changed for the better. A premium bond came up and, for once, it was one of ours. With the princely sum of one hundred pounds in his pocket, Dad was dragged, kicking and screaming, to the shops where Mum wasted it all on the latest thing in twin-tubs. She was delighted with it but the delight had worn off somewhat after twenty years when she still had the same old washing machine. This state of affairs was only rectified many years later, when Dad was made redundant. She pounced on his paltry pay-off and treated herself to an automatic.

With the Premium Bond money spent, Dad gave up trying to make an honest living and decided to go back to flying, which he had been hoping to avoid. The whole family squeezed into Grampa M's Ford Consul, and we drove to Newtownards airfield where Dad was being interviewed for the position of Chief Flying Instructor. As we sat in the car waiting for him, we asked where he'd gone. Grampa said that he'd gone to see the big knobs. That shut us up. We couldn't believe there were bigger knobs out there than Dad's.

They offered him the post, so presumably his credentials were quite impressive after all. However, he'd also applied for a position at the flying school at Scone, Scotland, and this offered a higher salary. Although Mum and Dad were reluctant to leave their native Ulster once again, the need for some decent money coming in forced their hand, and we were soon back on the road.

Dad set off for Bonny Scotland soon afterwards, and we prepared to join him later, when he had some accommodation ready.

"It's a braw, bricht, moonlit nicht the noo," Grampa M taught us to say in readiness for our new life in Scotland.

Armed with this useful expression, we took a tearful farewell, and set out on our travels once again.

CHAPTER 6

THE DAWN OF LIBERATION

Gypsies take their own homes, friends and extended families around with them and so do not suffer from the same sense of dislocation as we did on our constant travels.

"Home is where your mother is," Dad would say sagely if we ever asked or complained.

"Well where is she then, Dad?" we'd ask in reply.

"Ah…ehm…she must be down the bingo again."

In truth though, Mecca was never our home. Although Mum had always wanted to go to bingo, Dad forbade it. He was scared that she would become an addicted gambler, alcoholic, and loose woman if she ever ventured anywhere near such a den of iniquity. She was, in fact, in the kitchen, washing nappies. This was rather odd as we'd all grown out of nappies a long time before, but old habits die hard. When Dad confronted her about this odd behaviour, Mum got round the problem by falling pregnant again - but more of that later.

Everywhere I have ever lived, I have had a different

accent from those around me – even members of my own family. Within two weeks of arriving in Scotland, I overheard Little Harold saying to a new-found friend, "Och, I'm awa hame tae fetch ma bates, Angus." This turned out to be something to do with going home for his football boots. By the time that I had come anywhere near to mastering such an advanced level of the Scottish accent, we were on our way to England, following once again in the itchy footsteps of our father. But that was still some time in the future.

Harold, with his need to be one of the lads, was nearly as quick as Little Harold to pick up new accents. Jock, like myself, was slow to do so. Mum's accent always remained Belfast, but softened over the years of exile. Dad's accent varied depending on to whom he was talking, and whether or not it was on the phone. He could swear away in the best bog-Irish or put the Queen to shame with his telephone voice. Liverpudlians and Geordies would always be answered in their own dialects, and Germans were treated to the English language but in a guttural German accent delivered with a venom that even Hitler never quite surpassed at the Nuremberg rallies. For reasons known only to our father, the French, Belgians, Dutch and Danes, were also barked at in this German accent. He reserved his Welsh accent for Indians, Pakistanis and, to our astonishment, the Welsh.

He had a variation for talking to the Welsh though and usually spoke total gibberish that he would make us practice for months before going on holiday in Wales. "Leerapoke, larapoke, larabeean beeanowan, owansuli suli sac, macanaplatt," we were taught to reply to any Welshman who had the audacity to speak his own language in his own country. It did tend to spread widespread confusion, which kept Dad happy as that was his main goal in life.

Some years later, when I was living in Wales, I took a leaf out of Dad's book and learned to say, "Mae'n ddrwg gen i, ond dwi ddim yn siarad Cymraeg." ("Sorry old chap, but I don't speak a word of the lingo.") Again this confused anyone speaking to me in Welsh as they're not used to being spoken to in Welsh by a non-Welsh speaker.

The strange accents that we had at various times inevitably led to lots of fights, as children will not accept anyone who is different from them – at least not until they've had a good scrap. I had thought that we might be able to avoid this process in Scotland as Grampa M had taught us the Scottish accent before we left Belfast.

At lunchtime on the first day at our new school, I met up with Jock and Harold for mutual protection and we waited for the clans to gather. We didn't have long to wait. We were soon surrounded by curious and hostile local kids. I wasn't worried. I had my trump card to play.

"It's a braw, bricht, moonlit nicht the noo," I ventured.

We spent the rest of the day beating off attacks.

The Scots love scrapping. Even those that don't love it, do it anyway – perhaps to keep warm in the long, cold winters. In the past I'd needed to look for fights but in Scotland there were more than enough to go around and occasionally I over-booked, leaving some poor little soul standing around in the cold, waiting for his turn to have a go at me.

To try to avoid this sort of sad situation arising, they had a 'claiming' system. If you wanted to fight someone you would say, "You're claimed, Jimmy!" (The 'Jimmy' was optional.) After school, when you turned up at the allotted location for your fight, if you had claimed, or had been claimed by, more than one person, then the first claimant was entitled to the first go no matter who turned up earliest. In cases of gross over-booking (which were not rare) there would often be scraps over who had the right to fight next. The Scots don't like hanging around in queues when they could be punching someone.

The sheer quantity and viciousness of the fights took the fun out of it. I learned to be more patient and started to react to nasty situations instead of creating them. After Scotland, I only fought when I had to.

Even Jock learned to take care of himself in Scotland. He had no choice. "I'm sorry old chap but I'd rather go home for my tea than engage in a bout of fisticuffs," didn't cut it with the Scots, and they came at him from all sides. He'd always been a big lad and that had often saved him from being picked on in the past but the Scottish kids saw it as a challenge. He had to learn how to convert his size and strength into making people fall over. He learned, but he never enjoyed it.

Any thought that having a big brother at the school would let me get away with cheeking older boys was quickly dispelled when Henry Nearne caught me up the jacksie with a well-aimed winkle picker. He caught me dead centre and I was walking on tiptoes for a week. It

117

didn't half hurt! The safety lobby, when looking at producing pedestrian-friendly bonnets on cars, should also consider arse-friendly toecaps on boots.

When my father was a boy, he had similar problems with his accent as we were experiencing. As he was an only child, his upwardly-mobile mother persuaded his father that they could afford to send him to public school. The poor wee lad turned up at Petora, a posh boarding-school in Northern Ireland, with a broad Belfast accent. The other children, and the masters as well, picked on him until his enunciation, accent, and so on, had changed to mimic their own. He was reading a passage from a book in class one day and he read aloud that he had been 'misled'.

"Misled?" cried the outraged teacher. "'MISLED'? You mean 'misled', boy. 'MISLED'."

I can't help feeling that this story loses something in the written word. Never mind.

On the subjects of gypsies and fighting, a gypsy lad beat up Harold, knocking out one of his world-famous front teeth. Although secretly pleased, I joined in the gathering of the clans and we went looking for the culprit. Unfortunately for me, I found him. He beat me up as well. I was so ashamed that I had lost a fight that I never told anyone until about twenty years later when I was having a drink with my brothers. But by that time he had slipped away and they couldn't find him.

Gypsies also gave me the opportunity for my first appearance on telly. A TV crew were filming a documentary, 'From Country to Town', or some such nonsense. It showed the trials and tribulations of a Gypsy family trying to settle down in the big city. Not that Scone was a city, or even a town, but the title sounded catchier than, 'From Country to Another bit of Country.'

One scene of the documentary showed the youngest gypsy lad playing in a football match with his new-found friends. Spotting the cameras, and not wanting to miss an opportunity for fame and fortune, I nipped home, changed into my football gear, then went back and waited hopefully at the side of the pitch. My friends were furious (because they hadn't thought of it) and the gypsy lad was furious (because he hadn't a clue who I was). But to the Director it was a case of 'the more the merrier', and I was invited on for my football and television debut. I believe that I made the director's cut – in the bin.

When we first arrived in Scotland, we were living on a building site in Perth. Only a couple of houses had been completed at the time. Unfortunately for us, our house wasn't one of them. Construction sites make excellent playgrounds for children. They may be highly dangerous but they keep the kids quiet and out of their parents' hair for hours at a time. Dad would chuck us out the door at daybreak and not expect to see us again until dusk – or maybe he just didn't expect to see us again.

Did I say that it keeps them quiet? I think that 'occupied' would have been a more accurate word.

BOIYYYNNNnnnngggggGGGGG…!!!!

A loud, BOIYYYNNNnnnngggggGGGGGing sound reverberated around the site, drawing Mum and Dad to the window. Through the usual Scottish mist they could see a huge centipede backing away from a newly constructed bungalow. The centipede came to a brief stop and then, in a blur of movement, leapt forward, reaching maximum velocity as it hit the door of the bungalow.

BOIYYYNNNnnnngggggGGGGG … THWACK!!!

The door flew off its hinges.

The centipede retreated a few paces, then its body dropped to the ground leaving just the legs and several upright protrusions. As the mist cleared, Mum recognised four of the protrusions as her beloved sons.

Having dropped our battering ram, we entered the bungalow to explore. A few minutes later, to our surprise, Dad arrived to explore as well. We escaped through a back window, returned home at high speed, and were sitting as good as gold when he got back from his fruitless search. I say fruitless, but he had an armful of tools that the workmen had stored in the bungalow. He took them into safe-custody as the now doorless bungalow was no longer secure. That was his story and he was sticking to it!

After a couple more weeks working on the building site we started at Robert Douglas Memorial School in nearby Scone. I am sorry to say that I do not remember who Robert Douglas was. So much for memorials!

I was eight and a half years old, in Primary Four, and blessed with a Northern Irish accent. I say 'blessed' because this saved me on Bannockburn Day when the local children had the quaint little custom of beating up any English kids at the school. As a foreigner, I was grabbed by a bunch of the thicker lads who hadn't been paying attention in history or geography lessons. Careless of getting blood on his new suit, one of the teachers bravely waded through the scores of boys pummelling English lads, and rescued me. "He's Northern Irish, ye thick, wee bar stewards," he yelled as he pulled me to my feet. He threw them an English boy to keep them occupied as we made our escape through the bloodthirsty throng.

The teachers themselves were responsible for a lot of the anti-English feeling at the school because all the history we learned was about the cowardly English oppressor slaughtering innocent Scotsmen, or of the glorious, bloody victories where the brave Scots slaughtered wicked Englishmen (who, of course, were *not* innocent). Music lessons were full of patriotic Scottish songs – and patriotic Scottish songs are invariably anti-English songs. And nothing stirs the blood like a good, bloody song.

The Irish might shoot the English every now and then, but in a good-natured way. They like them far better than the Scots do. They only really attack them out of habit rather than because of any real ill-feeling towards them. The Scots, on the other hand, have a genuine antipathy for the English, which is seldom found in Ireland where they're more likely to blame the government than the people themselves for any past naughtiness.

Another odd thing in Northern Ireland is that the loyalist, 'British', Protestants dislike the English more than do the republican, 'Irish', Catholics. This despite the fact that in recent times the former waved Union Jacks at them while the latter waved Kalashnikovs. This tends to confuse your average Englishman who sometimes doesn't feel appreciated and calls for Northern Ireland to be thrown out of the United Kingdom. This wouldn't solve the problem. What is really needed is for Northern Ireland, Scotland and Wales to get together and throw *England* out while the Scots still have their North Sea gas supplies (hang on – they're running out); the Welsh still have their coal mines (hang on – they're all shut); and Northern Ireland still has its ship building and textile industries (hang on – the shipyards and mills have closed). Alright, the English can stay for now.

As our building site grew steadily smaller, and the new-built houses closed in around us at a faster rate than my brothers and I could demolish them, we decided to move to a more secluded spot on Stormont Road in Scone, close to our school and to Dad's place of work.

Strangely enough I have always moved to streets and towns with some connection to where I had been before or where I would end up. For example, I moved to Stormont Road from Northern Ireland, where Stormont is the parliament; at school in Scotland, I was put into a House called 'Mansfield', a town where I later went to work in England; I moved from Chesterfield Road in Bristol, to Chesterfield in Derbyshire, where I lived on Redvers Buller Road, Redvers 'Buller' being my Grandad's nickname. I could go on (and on and on), but I'm even boring myself so I can only guess how you must be feeling.

Our home on Stormont Road was the first and last new house I have ever lived in. It didn't agree with me. It had floor-vented hot air central heating which I believe was the original cause of the cold I have had ever since. One of my teachers said that I really should get my guitar sorted out. I told Dad, who had recently bought one for Jock, but he said it was a different sort of catarrh. I wasn't worried what sort it was as long as it was bigger than Jock's. Dad eventually came up with the goods years later, on my twenty-first birthday. For the time being I had to content myself with the odd furtive twang on Jock's guitar, accompanied by the odd nasal twang of my own catarrh-ridden vocals.

We were playing in the woods with some friends after we'd lived in Scone for only a few weeks. Harold grew tired of the game of commandos we were playing, and wanted to go home. I was enjoying myself and didn't want my young brother ruining my fun, so I told him to go home on his own.

"But I don't know the way," he whined.

We were only fifty yards from our house.

"Just follow the burn upstream," I told him. "You can't miss the road."

I turned away and didn't notice him heading downstream. He missed the road by about six miles. When I eventually got home, there was no sign of Harold. Once again the neighbours were out beating the woods and dragging the streams, looking for him. With it being Scotland, they charged a small fee of course.

I was in the doghouse for my part in getting him lost. This really annoyed me, and the dog wasn't too pleased either. Harold was only one year younger than me, and if a seven year-old was daft enough to go downstream when

I had clearly said upstream, then I thought we were well rid of him.

A couple of old tinkers lived deep in the woods, and eked out a living by selling pegs and lucky heather, with the old sales ploy of a curse thrown in for anyone refusing to buy any. The husband strode about in a tattered kilt playing the bagpipes (the man played, not the kilt), as his wife hawked their wares. This tended to speed up sales as he made up for in volume what he lacked in ability. Everyone wanted shot of them quickly. Now this couple were not popular in the neighbourhood. There were daft stories going around about them stealing children and so on, although, oddly, no one we knew seemed to have had one stolen. When the search party came across them in the woods, Dad approached them, asking if they'd seen Harold, and inviting them to join the search. The good citizens of the village were horrified. They were of the opinion that confessions should be beaten out of them as to what they'd done to the innocent young lad and where they'd hidden his remains.

Dad's approach turned out to be very useful over the years as Harold proved to be an expert at getting lost. On several occasions in the future, Harold was escorted from the woods, accompanied by a horrible, ear-bashing skirl, as the tinkers piped him home. So much for the locals' theory of them stealing children -with our lot, they couldn't get them back home quick enough.

Luckily, on this occasion, Harold hadn't deviated from the stream (which is odd because he deviates from almost everything else), and so the search party eventually found him, cold, wet and bedraggled, just before dusk. When we got back home he was treated to a big bowl of soup, while I was in the soup and treated to a lecture on responsibility and the art of giving clear directions.

Dad had a bit of a cheek criticising anyone else's sense of direction, as his own wasn't that good. He set off to walk to work one morning, with a brisk wind in his face. He'd got about half a mile down the road when he stopped to light his pipe, turning his back on the wind as he did so. He then carried on walking and, fifteen minutes later, found himself back home. He'd forgotten to turn around again after he'd lit his pipe.

After Harold's misadventures in the woods, Dad decided that we all needed some survival training. Throughout that summer we were taken into the forest each weekend and taught woodcraft. He bought each of us a fine collection of knives – fishermen's knives, sheath knives, and Swiss army knives. By the end of the summer we were nearly as well-armed as the local kids.

Dad taught us to make snares, lay traps, and fish with just a line and a hook kept in a small tin along with some chocolate and matches. We had 'Wayfarer' shoes with a compass concealed in the heel. He also taught us to build bivouacs for shelter in case we were caught out in the woods for a night.

We dutifully built our little, fern-covered shelters and spent a night in them, not wanting to hurt Dad's feelings by letting him know that we could build log cabins that made his bivouac look like an Aussie outhouse compared to a Georgian mansion, or that we had already trapped and eaten half the wildlife of the surrounding woodlands.

Next item on Dad's survival agenda was swimming lessons. These were truly horrific. The enthusiastic group of water-loving kids that set out eagerly for that first, fateful lesson, was soon reduced to a snivelling bunch of hydrophobes who would go to any lengths to avoid these sessions. Our ordeal was not helped by the fact that our swimming instructor (Dad) could not swim. Once again the library and his imagination were the chief sources of his inspiration and our torture. We were guinea pigs for his trial and error (mainly error) techniques – trial by ordeal. At first we were convinced that he had accidentally taken out a book on scuba-diving instead of swimming, but had forgotten the breathing apparatus. It was certainly a long time before we could swim with our heads actually above water.

Dad's main instrument of torture was a long pole (long enough to prod us away from the safety of the side of the pool) with a large canvass hoop attached to one end. Each child in turn, squealing and struggling, was slotted into this hoop and swung over the side into the deep end of the pool. We were then ordered to commence swimming as Dad, walking along the side of the pool and 'supporting' us from the drier end of the pole, read aloud from his book, *The Art of Chinese Water Torture*.

This instrument was ostensibly to enable him to keep our heads above water while we were practising our swimming strokes. In reality he used it to dunk us under if we swallowed a mouthful of water and, coughing and spluttering, stopped attempting to swim. He'd also dunk us under the water if we cried, complained, passed wind, or peed in the pool. As we did all of these things frequently during a lesson, we tended to spend more time underwater than above it.

We dreaded these sessions. I remember one Wednesday evening, standing in the doorway with Harold and Little Harold, our swimming togs wrapped in towels and tucked under our sweaty armpits, as we waited for Dad and Jock to get back from town and take us to 'The Pool'. (Those two words still make me shudder.) They had set off on Dad's scooter but arrived home in a taxi, several of their limbs in plaster. A car had pulled out in front of them, forcing them up the kerb. The scooter had remained on the road while they travelled, unaccompanied, along the pavement for several yards. A brick wall had eventually brought them to a halt. How we cheered when we realised that Dad was in no fit state to take us to the swimming baths. The taxi driver took one horrified look at our grinning faces then shot off without waiting to be paid. Unfortunately, their wounds healed all too soon and we were dragged back to the watery chamber of horrors for more 'tuition'.

Dad promised that once we could swim a length of the pool unaided, then we would never again be slung in the sling, and the sling would be slung. He had been teaching us something vaguely resembling the breaststroke, but I was still several months away from perfecting it to a lengths worth. I could not face another six months of the sling. I had to swim that length. Closing my eyes and steeling myself to overcome my fears and attempt the

127

impossible, I plunged into the deep end and improvised. A desperate combination of techniques – floating, farting, and doggy-paddling, combined with taking a few steps along the bottom each time I sank – eventually carried me, half dead, to the other end of the pool. I had done it! I had travelled the length of the pool unaided and the hated sling was banished from my life. From then on I took great pleasure in watching my brothers being slung about as I happily splashed around in the shallow end, sling free.

When, finally, we could all swim well enough to survive most situations, even in the water, we were plunged back into the woods for map-reading exercises and forced marches. Time had immunised Dad to public opinion, and the opportunity to use a bit of alliteration proved too much of a temptation for him to resist. He used his dreaded middle name for the first time ever and named us, 'Humbert's Hikers'. The name was boldly festooned on our backpacks as we hobbled around the countryside in Dad's not inconsiderable wake.

He equipped us with knapsacks and boots, then led us towards the edge of the denser, darker, unexplored forest to the rear of our house. Crossing a field as we marched towards the woods, Dad spotted some Highland Cattle in the treeline. These horned and hairy herbivores were allowed to wander semi-wild, bulls and all.

Dad panicked. "RUN!" he yelled at the top of his voice.

We all stopped dead, looking around the empty field, and then back at him. He was definitely agitated about something but we had no idea what. Our inaction stirred him to fury.

"RUUUNN!" he yelled again, murder written on his contorted face.

My brothers were taking no chances. They didn't know why or where, but they started running.

I stood my ground. "Where to?" I enquired politely.

He lowered his face to within an inch of mine.

"RRRUUUUUUUUUUUUUUUUUUUNNNNNN!!!" he explained helpfully at the top of his voice, blowing jets of Brylcreem from my hectored hair and leaving it standing erect as a guardsman's busby.

It dawned on me that, if I didn't start running, he was going to kill me. On the other hand, I had no intention of accidentally running straight into whatever it was that was so perturbing my previously imperturbable father. I opted for a compromise.

"Where? Where? Where?" I panted, as I ran in circles around him.

He finally steered me by the ear to the nearest hedge and hurled me over, then turned to face the expected highland charge. The cattle were grazing peacefully at the edge of the woods, tactfully ignoring the frantic activity that their appearance had caused.

We regrouped on the other side of the hedge and, battered but unbowed, plunged into the dark forest for our hike. There were paths marked on Dad's map, and so we followed them, even though they didn't exist. His map-reading ability was not to be questioned and we had to plough through any obstacle if it was on the 'path' he was following on the map. We were finally brought to a halt by a massive tree, slap bang in the middle of our route.

Dad shook his compass a few times, glared at it, rechecked his map, then concluded that it had been drawn up in an office by some jumped-up little official who had never ventured into a forest in his life. Eventually, after much pleading on our part and swearing on Dad's, we were allowed to walk around the tree.

We arrived home from our three-mile hike, utterly exhausted, having covered over seventeen miles. Mum cleaned our cuts and scratches, treated Little Harold's sunstroke, and glowered at Dad, who was sitting at his bureau, happily planning our next expedition.

Our house in Scone was in a delightful setting, surrounded on three sides by woodlands. By the time we left however, much of it had been built on, or burnt down by careless children. As well as aiding in the latter matter, my brothers and I were also active in the first. We ran a major building program, pinching Forestry Commission logs and dragging them off, tied to the back of our bicycles, before humping them overland to clearings suitable for making log cabins.

Our gang huts were masterpieces of construction technology. They would have stood for longer than most of the houses being built in the sixties had it not been for the law-abiding citizens of the nearby estate, and for Billy McNutter and his gang. The law-abiding citizens spotted our headquarters, a large, solid, log-built structure which was too close to the road to hide it from prying eyes. They quickly realised that it was built from pilfered Forestry Commission logs, and so they dutifully knocked it down and carried the wood back to their housing estate where they were building a massive bonfire for Guy Fawkes Night. Billy McNutter and his gang, on the other hand, had a search and destroy policy whereby they would scour the woods for any sign of us or our gang huts. They'd decimate either on sight.

'Billy McNutter' is not his real name. I changed it to protect the innocent – *me*! His gang were three or four years older than us so we had to use slightly different tactics to them in our raids into their territory. For example, if we found one of their tree huts we would hide and wait until we were sure they were not around before climbing up and knocking it down. If they discovered one of our tree huts, they would hide until they were sure we were in it before climbing up and knocking it down.

On one occasion, after a successful foray against a well-camouflaged gang hut of theirs, we were winding our way back through the thick undergrowth, heading for the safer, more familiar end of the woods by our street, when we were ambushed. They had discovered their recently smashed up hut and, realising who the culprits probably were and what direction we would be heading in, they'd set off in hot pursuit.

This was their neck of the woods and a few shortcuts brought them to the main track back to our patch, at a point somewhere ahead of us. As we hurried along, we were too busy casting worried looks behind us for any sign of pursuit, to notice them hiding in the bushes either side of us. As we hurried past, they sprung their trap.

With blood-curdling yells they leapt out on us. We

shouldn't have stood a chance, but fear lends wings to sweaty feet and most of our gang shot off into the bushes and disappeared within seconds. There were two however, who did not feel fear and were therefore too slow to escape. I was too daft to be afraid and Jock believed that he could reason with them and appeal to their sense of fair play. They would not attack a younger boy, outnumbered ten to one, would they? Surely not! He was soon reasoning from a horizontal position, face down in the mud, as they stuck the boot in.

Billy and most of his gang ran off after our fleeing friends, but three stayed behind, one holding Jock down while the other two kicked him. So far I had been overlooked. Perhaps I was too small for even these bullies to bother with – beneath their attention. The thought rankled. As I watched them kicking and thumping my big brother, I became more and more enraged. No one was going to ignore *me* and get away with it!

I hurled myself onto the back of the nearest assailant, clamping on hadake-jime, a stranglehold that Dad had taught me. Choking and spluttering, he tried desperately to shake me off, but I held on like a limpet, the strangle squeezing tighter and tighter. As he started to turn blue, the other two let go of Jock in order to prise me off their friend. They laughed at him as he feverishly sucked in great lungfuls of air in between spluttering threats at me. They were so amused that he'd been beaten up by a little kid that they let us go, and Jock and I made good our escape before he'd got enough breath back to give chase.

When we eventually met up with the others, we

discovered that only James had been caught. He was the nearest thing we had to a gang leader, so Billy McNutter had roughed him up quite badly and he was not a pretty sight. Mind you, he was never a pretty sight. Although God had not exactly blessed him in the first place, James was determined to have his features rearranged into even stranger patterns and picked fights with anyone and everyone.

Jock had several run-ins with James and, while none of them were conclusive as neither of them ever conceded defeat, Jock took a battering from the first few tussles. However, as Jock became more used to the noble art of scuffling, which did not come naturally to him, and also as his rate of growth continued at the same phenomenal pace as it had done since his birth, he eventually began to get the better of James, whose attacks gradually diminished in frequency and then died away altogether after a little incident. One fateful summer's day, Jock had finally had enough of James. In a move that impressed even Harold and me with its implicit beauty, simplicity, and total lack of fair play, Jock caught him full in the gob with a galvanised steel dustbin lid. His head still hadn't stopped reverberating by the time he had staggered home.

To James's horror his dad stamped round to our house to complain. Recognising the 'disgruntled parent' demeanour as James's father marched up our driveway, Dad shouted up the stairs, "John. Get down here!"

I arrived at the door just as James's father stormed in. "Your Jock has just…"

"You mean, John," Dad interrupted him.

"I mean, Jock," shouted the man.

Dad's ears pricked up in interest.

"He hit my James in the face with a dustbin lid!"

Dad shook his head in disappointment. "No, you definitely mean, John."

"It was, Jock," the angry parent yelled.

Eyebrows raised, Dad turned to me. Reluctantly I nodded in agreement. I hated the thought of Jock getting all the credit.

A huge, proud and satisfied grin gradually spread across Dad's astonished face as this information slowly sank in. All those frustrating years of trying to get Jock to fight dirty had finally paid off. Try as he would, he couldn't keep the delighted beam off his face.

This didn't go down well with James's father. "What are you going to do about it?" he demanded.

"Jock," called Dad, fatherly pride etched in every word, "Get down here now, son."

An explanation for his behaviour was demanded, and given with a candour that had me even more jealous. Apparently, James had hidden up a tree and pished on him when he walked below.

Before hurrying off to beat his son for pishing on Jock, James's father still demanded that Jock be punished for bin-lidding his son. Dad assured him that he would be.

"That's my boy," Dad said proudly as he administered a token caning for this misdemeanour. He also put Jock's pocket money up to show there were no hard feelings and he actually approved of what he'd done.

Now that James had given up on Jock, he hit Harold

instead. Harold came in crying and, as Jock was out at the time, as the eldest brother present I was honour bound to go out and do battle for the family name. James had had the audacity to hit him in our own front garden, and was still there preening himself when I rounded the corner.

I was not looking forward to the encounter as I had seen him in action on a number of occasions, and he was a nasty piece of work. He was confident as well because we had fought before when Dad had put boxing gloves on us and set us on one another for his afternoon's entertainment. Being older and stronger than me, James had come out an easy winner, but this time it was for real – which is a totally different matter. I also had home advantage and was genuinely furious that he'd had the audacity to hit Harold in our own garden. That was *my* job.

As James pumped himself up for the customary pre-fight ritual of flinging insults and building up courage, I hurled myself straight at him. Taken by surprise, he went down under a flurry of blows. I followed him to the ground, sat on him, and continued to batter him.

It had all been so easy that I began to prematurely congratulate myself and I lost the anger and sense of purpose that had allowed me to the get the better of him in the first place. Never a quitter, James began to fight back.

I had lost interest by now but continued to sit on him and give him the odd whack, just for form's sake. He eventually managed to roll me off and, as he got on top of me and raised his fists, him all bloody and me without a mark on me, a sudden, devious plan entered my head.

"I give in," I said.

It was perfect. He was black and blue while I hadn't been touched. I was more than happy for things to remain that way. If he told anyone that he had beaten me, they would take one look at his battered face and not believe a word of it. He could hardly say, "You should see the other guy," when there wasn't a mark on me. It was a master plan. I almost felt sorry for him as I could hear the cogs of his tiny brain whirring, and the pained and puzzled expression on his battle-scarred face was sad to behold as he struggled to make sense of the situation.

His face cleared. He'd worked it out. "Oh, no you don't," he snarled, and laid into me.

We fought on for a time, neither getting the better of the other, until his mother came out and shouted him home for his tea. We shook hands on an honourable draw, but his tactical withdrawal meant that I was left in possession of the battlefield, and therefore, technically, the winner. I was glad that it had finished that way and not by the sneaky victory from defeat that I'd tried to manufacture on the spur of the moment. That way there would have been unfinished business. This way honours were even, and we never fought each other again.

Despite James's ugly face, and his sister's resemblance to him, I fell for her – literally. It was her who had set fire to the tree that time outside the scout hut.

We did exciting things together, like playing commandos, wrestling, and kissing when no one was looking. Alas, it was not to last. After a couple of days, as she grew older and less inclined to be one of the lads, Jock

136

noticed that she was female and took a shine to her. Flattered by the attentions of an older boy, she dumped me and ran off with him. I wasn't worried. I was more interested in playing in the woods and searching for rival gang huts.

Jock drifted away from his brothers at this stage. He found a new set of sophisticated friends who did not just want to mess about in the woods or on the building sites, and he began to allow older women, like Big Morag, to take advantage of him when Liz wasn't looking.

This was in the late sixties, at the height of Flower Power, and Liz was determined to make Jock more 'with it'. Little did she realise that, with Big Morag around, he was rarely without it. She tried to persuade him to grow his hair long, wear a suede jacket with tassels, and buy some flared trousers. She was unsuccessful. Dad was even more determined that we kept our trousers straight, and our hair short, Brylcreemed and slicked back. Our suede jackets remained in the shop window.

With Mum's collaboration, we staged a minor rebellion against Dad's tyranny when he was away on a course for the weekend. We did not have enough time to grow our hair long but at least we got two days growth in, which was longer than we normally had before he got his clippers out. We also attempted to grow whiskers but we only managed two between us, and they were growing out of a birthmark on my right arm. However, we did manage to go on a shopping trip with Mum. Our flares jutted out proudly in front of us as we swaggered and swished our way homewards that glorious afternoon.

At home, we waited anxiously for the moment of truth, when Dad got back from his travels. As expected, they both arrived at the same time.

As the key turned slowly in the lock, like a depth charge scraping down the side of a submarine, we looked nervously at each other, waiting for the coming explosion. Huddled together in the living room we subconsciously formed a square with our flares pointing outwards, ready to repulse enemy cavalry.

The front door creaked open. A footstep in the hall. We panicked and broke. It was every boy for himself as we bolted for the bedroom, tripping over each other's flares as we ran, and trampling Little Harold underfoot.

With the bedroom door shut tight behind us, we got our breath back and regrouped. Mum sat Dad down in the living room with a nice, relaxing cup of cocoa, then came to rally the dispirited troops. She sent me in first. The forlorn hope. The first wave. The cannon fodder. She told me it was because my drab, brown, moderately flared cords, were the least likely to send Dad off on one when compared to the multi-coloured, voluminous selection on offer. But then there is always a rational explanation, isn't there? They never tell you it's because you're expendable.

Perhaps my attire *was* the least likely to offend Dad. Nevertheless, when I entered the room shortly after the leading edge of my flares, a thin jet of cocoa sprayed out from between his tightly compressed lips.

Harold, in his bright red, seven feet wide flares, was saved until last. At the sight of him, Dad turned a funny colour and his teeth gnashed ominously, but he said nothing. For once in his life he'd been struck speechless.

It was a major victory for us, but that night the clippers came out, and the next day we were packed off to school with more grease than ever on what was left of our hair. Not even the hairs on my birthmark were spared. At least he had the decency to shave them off. I'd had visions of him slicking them back with a central parting.

By the time we were allowed to grow our hair long and not plaster it back fifties-style, everyone else was cutting theirs short and Brylcreem was back in fashion. So much for the swinging sixties. The only tripping we ever did was over the ends of our flares.

While Jock was thinking about dropping out, and trying to find something to drop out of, the rest of us carried on with what kids are best at. Back on the construction sites, we were causing chaos. The fields behind our house which swept up to the woods some eight hundred yards away (it was a big house), were now in the process of being built upon, which was a shame. We felt that it was our duty to slow down and disrupt this destruction of the environment, not so much from the green point of view as from the natural, instinctive, vandalistic tendencies common in young boys.

We were not destructive for the sake of it, as vandals might be, but because of the marvellous opportunities that unsupervised building sites provided. There were nails, felting and timber with which to build gang huts. There were ready-made ones in the form of half-finished houses. There were bricks and piles of dried clumps of mud, and trenches dug for foundations. The mud and bricks provided the ammunition that we threw at the enemy who were cowering in the trenches, waiting to attack when we tired and the bombardment diminished in intensity.

These mud fights were deadly at the height of the summer when the mud had hardened like rock, but they were fairly deadly all year round as some individuals cut out the middle man and just used rocks. Once, as I raised my head over the parapet to pick out a likely target, Andy McKinney caught me square in the mouth with a fist-sized stone disguised in a thin layer of mud. My lips swelled up to at least half the size of Leslie Ash's.

As I lay there in a daze, my concerned brothers and friends gathered around me. Taking advantage of my helpless state, they crammed me into a large section of concrete pipe and rolled me down a hill. I came to a painful and confused stop when it hit a JCB at the bottom.

The building sites even provided us with giant dodgems. We once found a nine-ton dumper with the keys in the ignition and the whole gang piled onto it. James took the controls and managed to start it up. We'd travelled about three yards when we realised that James wasn't the best of drivers. We all leapt overboard leaving the captain to go down with his ship. As he hurtled around the site, we realised that he had no idea how to stop the thing, so we did the decent thing. We went home and left him to it.

The builders were not as keen on our activities as we were, and they often played chase or hide-and-seek with us. On one occasion we were mucking about in a nearly-completed house when the agent arrived to show a young couple around. James and I were downstairs while the others were messing around upstairs. Footsteps and voices sounded outside, and I overtook James as we raced up the stairs out of the way. We reached the top just in time to see the end of the loft-ladder disappearing through the attic hatchway. Faces smirked down on us from above before our 'friends' dropped the hatch cover firmly into place, leaving us stranded.

Scrambling back downstairs again, we heard the door creaking open. As I looked around frantically for a hiding place, I noticed James trying to squeeze himself in over the hot water boiler in the tiny airing cupboard. He had no chance of succeeding, but I stopped for a few seconds to enjoy his contortions before pointing out the trapdoor in the cloakroom floor. I knew about it because the house was virtually the same design as our own, and *our* trapdoor had come in handy as the last resting place of Dad's cane. He never discovered its whereabouts but he bought himself an even swishier one and, as he swished, we wished that we had left well alone and not hidden his old one.

In the meantime, as the salesman showed an enthusiastic young couple into the house, James managed to disentangle himself from the boiler and followed me underground. We only just made it. Their footsteps soon sounded right over our heads. We could clearly hear the sales-patter of the agent, and the appreciative 'oohs' and 'aahhs' of the prospective buyers.

Worried that they might look down the trapdoor, we squirmed away under the floor to another area. We lay in nervous silence for a few minutes then footsteps sounded overhead again as they entered the room above.

Safe in our new hiding place our courage slowly returned as our initial fear of being caught receded. We could hear every word that was being spoken above and we started to enjoy the situation. I picked up a stone and scraped it along the bottom of the floor.

"What was that?" asked a worried voice from above.

"What was what? I didn't hear anything." The salesman's voice had a nervous edge to it.

I gave it a minute until James and I had our giggles under control, then I scraped the floor a second time.

"There it was again!" came a high-pitched woman's voice. "It must be rats!"

"Oh no, I don't think so." The salesman's voice was decidedly shaky. "It doesn't seem to me…"

James decided to lend a hand to the proceedings. Never one to do things by half, he picked up a broken brick and nearly put it through the floor, he bashed it that hard.

There was a shriek from above, followed by rapidly retreating footsteps. The salesman's frantic pleading, "But…but…but…!" gradually died away to a quiet but heart-felt, "Shit!" as the door slammed above.

There were a few missing breeze blocks in the walls under the floor, and we wriggled out through a gap and made a run for it in case the salesman decided to investigate, though my guess is that he ran the young couple a close second in his hurry to get out of the house.

We were well known to the local Bobby who used to have little chats with us about raiding orchards, re-siting Forestry Commission property, and poaching, amongst other things. He called it poaching - we called it guddling. Guddling is basically tickling trout as a means of fishing with the hands. The more expert guddlers would find fish hiding in slow-moving water under overhanging rocks, tickle them to put them into a sort of trance, and then pull them out. I dispensed with the tickling bit, and merely cornered the fish and tried to grab them and drag them out. My thinking was severely flawed and the technique was rarely successful. Some of the guddlers though, were very good, and could catch as many fish as their mothers ordered.

Scrumping apples was another pastime that we enjoyed. It was almost expected of kids of our age. The older generation would look on fondly as we raided an orchard, whimsically muttering, "Ah, that takes me back. When I was a lad…"

I had one unpleasant experience when on a scrumping expedition. The orchard that we intended to raid was quite a way away, so we commandeered some transport from a group of younger kids that were passing by. The raid was successful but, on the way back, I was having difficulties riding the bike I'd borrowed, as it was designed for a much smaller child. As we came down a steep hill, I got a wheel wobble and went straight over the handlebars, landing in a painful heap in the middle of the road. When I refused to ride the bike any further, some kind soul agreed to swap it for the scooter he was riding. I set off down the hill, hit a stone, and went straight over the handlebars for a second time in a row. I limped home, deftly avoiding a herd of angry parents who were not pleased with our transport policy, even though we'd returned the vehicles to their diminutive owners on completion of our mission.

The local bobby turned a blind eye to most of our activities, but he didn't like us slipping into the plantation and chopping down our own Christmas trees over the festive season – a little peccadillo not objected to by our parents. In fact tools like saws and axes, that were carefully locked away out of reach of destructive little hands for most of the year, would strangely turn up on driveways as the local kids were heading out to play in the woods around Christmastime. A cacophony of sawing and chopping reverberated around Scone at this time of year, but the parents were always well out of the way, with sound alibis.

We were once caught leaving the woods with a saw, but no tree. We had enough sense to hide the trees nearby before collecting them later, under cover of darkness. As the policeman questioned us, Douglas was squirming around, cutting his legs as he tried to shove the saw down the back of his trousers, out of sight. The bobby cruelly waited for him to finish before asking him to hand it over.

After years of harassing us for minor damage to the fir tree plantation, the powers-that-be bulldozed the lot and built on it for a profit. I hate vandalism.

As we were in Scotland, Mum decided to have another baby because she didn't have a Scottish one. Our family was a mini version of the United Kingdom. She'd have gone on to form the United Nations if Dad hadn't finally put two and two together and realised what was causing it.

He quickly put a stop to it after that.

Mum told us that she was pregnant and that there was a baby in her rapidly expanding belly.

Harold said, "Humph! I'll believe it when I see it."

Jock moaned, "Oh no! What will I tell my teacher?" (They always teased us about the number of our siblings passing through their classes. They couldn't seem to get away from us.)

Little Harold was enthusiastic, and squeaked, "We'll call him, Edward, and he can sleep with me."

My reactions to Mum giving birth had been changing over the years. I had advanced from my initial, "Yuch!" on seeing Harold, to a resigned, "Well, okay then, as long as we can call him Charly Bill," when Little Harold was born. So this time it was all old hat to me. I'd seen it all before. Or had I? The baby turned out to be... a girl!

We were in shock. We hadn't thought that Mum did girls. It took us twelve months to come to terms with it. It took Bon twelve years. She refused to accept that she was different from her brothers and this led to a few problems. Once, for example, Mum found her standing in a puddle of pee in front of the toilet. "I just wanted to do it like the boys," she cried.

For once, probably because I was quite a bit older than her, I was not jealous of the new-born baby. Before she reached talking age, which wasn't long, she mainly entertained us by bouncing in her baby-bouncer suspended in and open doorway. A few years earlier I might have taken pleasure from slamming the door and seeing how high she could really bounce, but I was mellowing in my old age and I merely looked on benevolently.

The baby-bouncer kept her entertained until she was nearing one-year-old, by which time she was beginning to walk and talk. This is when she came into her own in entertainment value, and we all competed for her attention. For the next few years she held centre stage, enthralling us with her pronunciation of words like, 'hyperploppymouse', 'ringtosserhouse', and her favourite tennis player, 'Jelly Bean King'. As her knowledge and her vocabulary increased, she began to treat us to fascinating pieces of information such as, 'Pigs are the cleanest animals on a farm – when they've been washed.' We nicknamed her, 'Bon', because she called herself 'Ush Bon' instead of Siobhan. Sugar was 'ushgar'.

For the first few years of her life, Bon was very nervous and clingy. She literally clung to Mum's skirts, and followed her everywhere around the house. She screamed the place down if Mum was ever more than an arm's length away from her.

She was terrified of nurses. Presumably this was because she had been born with jaundice and had undergone a series of blood transfusions as a small baby. For months afterwards the district nurse visited on a frequent basis, taking blood samples. Even as a baby, Bon recognised the nurse's uniform and associated it with the pain of a needle. She burst into tears at the sight of one.

As soon as she learnt to speak, Bon told Mum that she used to be her little sister, and that they lived in a small, round hut with no windows. Mum and Dad were convinced that this was proof of reincarnation. We thought it was proof that she was batty.

Bon had my temper, Jock's eloquent grasp of the English language, Harold's love of animals, and Little Harold's imagination. She often displayed all of these traits at the same time. Once when she was two years old, Mum took her to the local park. They were watching a squirrel playing with its nuts, when a gang of young yobs walked by. One of them said, "Let's set fire to that squirrel's tail." Two-year-old Bon wasn't standing for that. Drawing herself up to her full height of three feet, she broke free from Mum's grip, and ran at the boys, yelling, "Yah boo, yah boo, yah boo!" Luckily Mum caught up with her and dragged her away before she could savage the poor lads.

Grandpa W had a stroke so Mum took two-year old Bon with her to Belfast to see him in hospital. It was 1970 and 'The Troubles' had started. He was in the Queen Victoria Hospital so, from Granny's house on the Shankill, they had to walk through a tough, Republican area to get there. People were demonstrating outside the police station on the Springfield Road as they walked by, and it was noisy and intimidating, but Bon wasn't worried. When they'd finished their visit, Mum said to Bon, "Say 'bye-bye, Grampa'." She said, 'bye-bye Grampa', to every old man on the ward. It made their day. She then did the same as they walked back past the demonstration. It broke up peacefully.

When they got back to Scotland, Mum noticed that around 5pm each evening, Bon would have chocolate plastered round her face. She couldn't work out where she was getting it from, so one day, at the appointed time, she lay hidden, in waiting. Sure enough, at 5pm, Bon headed for the door (she couldn't even tell the time, but she knew). As Mum watched, a shadowy figure appeared outside the door and curmudgeonly, old James next door fed Bon chocolate through the letterbox.

Harold went down with whooping cough. Not wanting to be outdone by my little brother, I joined him. At first it was a bit scary and unpleasant, but we soon became used to it. I'd shout, "Bombs away!" every time I had to run to the toilet to be sick. It happened so often that I just treated it as part of normal life and didn't worry about it at all, unless Harold was already hanging over the toilet when I got there, in which case it could get a little messy.

Apart from the whooping and heaving, we had a wonderful time. We felt fine after the first couple of weeks, but were still infectious and so were not allowed to return to school. Bliss. The weather was gorgeous, and we delighted in lounging in the front garden, taunting our schoolmates on their way to or from school.

There was, however, one major blot on the landscape. Bon caught whooping cough from us. She was still a baby and had not been vaccinated. As she coughed and whooped, the veins stood out on her head and she turned various odd colours. My brothers and I were fascinated, but Mum and Dad, knowing how dangerous it was for a baby, found it terrifying. She was lucky to survive.

After recovering I still 'whooped' whenever I coughed, and this went on for several years until slowly fading away.

Sunday, in our household, was the day reserved for saving our souls. Mum and Dad dragged us out of our nice, warm beds at some ungodly hour, washed and scrubbed us, then forced us into horrible, smart, little outfits. We were half-choked by ties that Dad deliberately fastened too tight to deprive us of oxygen in order to slow us down and make us appear well-behaved in church. 'Children should be seen but not heard,' was one of Dad's favourite sayings. His wish came true on Sundays – we could hardly breathe, let alone speak. In this sedate (or sedated) state, half-dead from oxygen starvation, we would sit in a pew with our proud parents, gasping our way through a few hymns, until it was time for the children to leave the main church and go to Sunday school.

Once out of sight, off came our ties and, after a five minute lung-filling acclimatisation period, out came our true personalities. I achieved a certain notoriety by becoming the first member of the congregation to have a fist-fight at church. (I was first equal to be honest. The other boy had a hand in it as well, not to mention his foot.) After this incident, our Sunday school teacher was less inclined to encourage lively debate on bible stories, and stuck to more obscure passages that she hoped my Granny wouldn't have influenced me on.

My fame spread on presentation day when the minister called me up to the front of the church to receive a prize for my high attendance level. (I was dragged there, kicking and screaming, every bleeding week. Well kicking anyway – I couldn't scream because of the tie.) I accepted the gift (a bible) graciously, in front of my proud and beaming parents and the rest of the congregation. Then I spotted the pulpit. Tucking the bible down the back of my trousers, I leapt up, caught the rim of the pulpit and swung round it, hand over hand, to the far side. I then dropped to the floor and majestically swept back up the aisle to our pew, to appreciative applause from my brothers. I noticed that Mum and Dad were not beaming anymore. Mum was studiously studying the floor, and Dad was glaring at me with a look on his vengeful visage that spoke nothing of peace, piety and forgiveness, the subjects of the sermon.

The minister decided that he could use my stage presence, and press-ganged me into the choir. Before long my brothers had joined me and, on occasion, we strummed along to the hymns on our ukuleles. On one of these occasions we were discovered by a talent spotter and signed up for a stage career – playing at the annual general meeting of the church elders. This was an honour we shared with the organist and his extremely talented family who had hitherto done the gig on their own. What they had in cold-blooded musical talent, we countered with our hot-blooded, never mind the duff notes, enthusiasm.

Come the big night, Dad had us well-rehearsed and prepared, right down to drinking a honey cordial to soothe our throats and keep our singing sweet. The business meeting was still in progress when we arrived at the church hall. As the two families, the talented one and us, trooped across the stage to the changing rooms, there were appreciative 'oohs' and 'aahs' from the hall at the large variety of musical instruments everyone was carrying.

This descended into a meeting-disturbing burst of laughter as I brought up the rear with a shovel over my shoulder. (This was my prop for my big moment in 'Who Killed Cock Robin.' My line was ' "I," said the owl, "with my little trowel. I'll dig the grave." ' This confession was to be accompanied by an enthusiastic demonstration of digging, using the shovel in lieu of a trowel.)

On the night, Little Harold let the side down. As he couldn't play the ukulele, Dad had bought him a triangle. He had only one note to play all evening, this coming at the end of our very last song. All through the gig, Little Harold stood with his tinger poised high above his triangle, as he eagerly waited for his big moment. The longer the performance went on, the more the audience concentrated their attention on Little Harold, standing stock still, centre stage, tinger at the ready, but not a note yet played.

The tension mounted. The last song arrived and still the tinger hadn't descended. The audience leaned forward in their seats, all eyes on four-year old Little Harold. Was he going to hit the bloody thing or not?

The song ended. There was a long, pregnant pause as the rapt audience waited and waited, but still Little Harold stood poised, beads of sweat running down his face with the concentration, even though his cue had long since come and gone.

Eventually a few non-believers started to clap, thinking our performance was over, and then a loud, 'TINNNGG!' rang out above the smattering of polite applause. The house exploded in a roar of approval, and we were called back for an encore.

Applause does something to a person that banishes nerves in an instant. Our encore was drowned out by a demented Little Harold, playing his triangle like he was calling the cowboys in from the range for their evening chow. No amount of malevolent stares from his brothers could stop him, and he was still on stage, rattling away with his tinger, long after we'd packed up and the audience had gone home. I offered to fetch my shovel and shut him up, but Dad got to him first and dragged him, kicking and screaming but still tonking away like a demon, from the stage.

"But there's still someone listening," wailed Little Harold.

It was the caretaker, who slammed and locked the door firmly behind us as we left.

A more lucrative outlet for our musical ... 'Inclination', (I was about to say 'talent', but caught myself on), was 'guysing'. During the run-up to Halloween and Guy Fawkes Night, Scots kids, instead of running the protection racket of 'trick or treat' practised in England and America, knock on doors and sing for their sweets. Believe me the latter is far more unpleasant to the victims than the former. Those of you who have been plagued by carol singers at Christmas will have some idea of the distress that can be caused by unwanted warblers. But at least carol singing is restricted to a time of year when most of us are feeling festive and a little more charitable than usual, and their repertoire is limited to a few well-loved Christmas ditties. Now imagine the grim time as October is turning into November. The toil of everyday work is starting to grind you down again and your summer break is a fading memory. The weather has turned cold, wet and miserable. And you're skint, being caught between the expense of your summer holiday and saving for Christmas. Just as you have settled down in your favourite armchair and put your feet up in front of a roaring fire, 'Old MacDonald Had a Farm' is blasted through your letterbox at ninety decibels, with your milk bottles being kicked over in accompaniment to ensure that you have heard the guysers. This might be followed up with, 'El Solo Mio', to the sound of your dustbin lids being rattled raucously, with an encore of 'Tulips in Amsterdam', accompanied by your autumn blooms being fed through the letterbox one by one, until you open the door and pay up. If you are still ensconced in your lovely, warm chair by this stage, and have resisted all attempts to tempt you and your wallet to the front door, a lighted 'banger' might well find its way through the letterbox to join your precious flowers.

We used to turn up on people's doorsteps, with our little ukuleles in our hands, and stay and play until we were paid. That was our motto, and also the slogan we would chant through the letterboxes of the more reluctant households – 'We'll stay, and play, until you pay!'

After the first season of this, I became overcome with remorse and shyness, and refused to join my brothers in any future dastardly, nocturnal activities. Dad, who had been so violently against us 'trick or treating', was furious with me for refusing to join my brothers in their annual, musical mugging of the local populace. Every year he gave me a hard time, calling me a coward who was letting down his family. I dug my heels in and refused to give in to these tirades. I might have been a coward, but I was not going to let anyone bully me out of it.

I never quite grasped the subtle difference between 'guysing' and 'trick or treating' that stirred such violent feelings in my father, one way and the other. He did once explain that it was like an adult telling an untruth and a child lying; taxation and extortion; war and murder. I just couldn't see the difference.

CHAPTER 7

THE DAWN OF LIBERATION

Gordon was not one of my favourite people. He was an only child and a spoilt brat. His parents bought him an endless string of presents to make up for the fact that they were rarely around for him. We often seethed as we watched him deliberately smashing up toys that we would have given our eye teeth for. He also bought every number-one single in the pop charts, regardless of whether or not he actually liked the song. I thought this was a ridiculous, wasteful and pointless thing to do, and it annoyed the hell out of me. Now I wish I had my hands on that collection. It'll be worth a fortune.

Gordon did have his uses. Both of his parents worked and he was a 'latchkey kid' before they had been invented. This meant that, in the summer holidays, he had the house all to himself during the day. Well not quite all to himself. School holidays were party time at Gordon's.

The local Spar shop happily sold us bottles of cider on the production of the requisite ID. Any ID with the Queen's head on it, was quickly accepted. Armed with our bottles, scores of us descended on Gordon's house each summer, for wild, drunken orgies. When I say 'wild, drunken orgies', it may be a bit of an exaggeration. We could not afford enough cider to get drunk, and none of us was sure how to 'orgy' properly. But we *were* wild.

The more adventurous elements amongst us tackled Gordon's gin and port, hoping that his father would not notice the levels lowering. After one better than usual session, we had to top up the port bottle with water. Surprisingly, nothing was said. Either he was turning a blind eye, or the father's taste was as bland as the son's.

The girls seemed to instinctively have a better idea of how to orgy than us boys. Young ladies, rosy cheeks shining, flushed with their half glass of cider, ran around the house pulling down the shorts of any unsuspecting young lads who lingered too long without their backs to the wall. We were terrified. Naive as we were, we pulled them back up again, telling the girls to grow up.

The closest these parties came to becoming a real orgy was when Jock, who was fast approaching his teens, ended up in bed with a young lady of previously unblemished reputation. Luckily his magic underpants came to the rescue. Jock's growth spurts always kept him one step ahead of Mum's clothes shopping, and his underpants were stretched across him tighter than a nun's knees. He had to be greased and levered into them with a shoehorn each morning. On this occasion they stood firm (his underpants that is) and resisted all attempts to get in or out of them. Chastity won the day yet again.

One person who was not chaste (not with that spelling

anyway) was an older girl affectionately known as 'Monkey', on account of her good looks. She used to disappear into the woods with a startling variety of young men. We found this difficult to understand, as her face was definitely not her fortune. If it had been, then she would have been declared bankrupt.

In order to solve this mystery, Harold and I followed Monkey and her latest victim into the woods. We were both well-versed in creeping through woodland undetected, and neither Monkey nor Goofy, her equally large and facially-challenged escort, suspected our presence. However, they disappeared into a thick Rhododendron bush and we could not see what was happening. As the rustling from the bush became more and more frantic, and Goofy's squeals of pain or fear (we assumed it was one or the other) became louder and louder, curiosity overcame my natural caution. I fearlessly sent Harold in for a closer look.

I jumped a foot in the air as first Harold, and then Monkey, let out blood-curdling shrieks. A few seconds later, Harold burst into view again with Goofy, his trousers round his ankles and a huge knife in his hand, close on his heels. We made a rapid tactical withdrawal.

In this dignified race through the woods, Goofy was at a distinct disadvantage. With a seven-inch blade in his hand he dared not try to pull up his trousers while stumbling along at speed. Even if he got them up he would have been a brave man to zip them up in his angry state. We soon left him far behind but kept on running as we could hear him hopping along furiously, far to our rear. He

157

was hopping mad.

When we reached the road, we felt it was safe to stop for a breather. When Harold got his breath back he insisted that he had not been scared of Goofy – it had been the sight of Monkey naked that had made him scream.

Never again did we follow Monkey. If she enjoyed wrestling with half-naked, knife-wielding madmen, then that was her business. The mystery had been solved and we wanted nothing more to do with it.

Although he never again followed Monkey, Harold had not yet learned the lesson that strange noises emanating from bushes are best left uninvestigated. As he walked in the park one day, an angry buzzing, amidst shouts, laughs, and the sound of stones crashing through the undergrowth, drew him into another set of rhododendron bushes. As he entered, he was nearly knocked down by the previous occupants who were making a rapid exit.

Harold arrived in time to see the smashed wasp nest, just as the wasps saw him. They were not in a friendly mood. They attacked him and chased him as he ran home screaming. He presented himself in our living room, with a large number of wasps still around him and stinging for all they were worth.

I took in the situation at a glance and bravely jumped out the window. Luckily for me, it was open at the time. Jock, who would rather face a herd of stampeding elephants than stand up to an angry wasp (or even a slightly irritated one), narrowly beat me to it. Mum and Dad courageously stayed behind – Mum to defend her son, and Dad because the wasps were between him and the window.

Having cleared the wasps out of Harold's hair, Mum pulled off his jumper to discover several more underneath it, all still happily stinging away. One of these wasps flew up her skirt and stung her. This finally stung Dad into action and he jumped up just as quickly, but not quite so high, as Mum had done. Brandishing a rolled-up newspaper (I believe it was *The Sun*) he bounded after the guilty wasp, ignoring the rest of the swarm in his single-minded attack.

"Take that… and that," he yelled as he swiped at it. "How dare you sting my wife?"

However, it showed no remorse and so, single-handed, Dad knocked it to the floor and beat it to death with his improvised cudgel. He then turned on poor Harold, for throwing stones at a wasps' nest (which he denied). Only Harold's distressed state saved him from a beating as nothing, not even an indiscrete wasp, angered Dad as much as one of us declaring our innocence once he'd decided we were guilty.

Harold never had much luck with rhododendron bushes. One of our favourite games was climbing up trees that were surrounded by these bushy shrubs, then leaping off, letting the rhododendrons break our falls. But Harold always managed to find the gaps. If there was a nice, leafy-looking patch then you could bet your life that, if Harold leapt at it, there would be nothing underneath the top layer of leaves but fifteen feet of empty space, and a hard landing awaiting. He ended up flat on his back, gasping and staring at the sky, more often than Monkey.

We enjoyed the winters in Scotland – especially Harold,

as there were no wasps around. There were lovely great snowdrifts that we sank in up to our thighs. We tied planks of wood to your feet, and convinced ourselves we were skiing. We tobogganed down snow-covered hills, or skated on the ice-bound pond.

The most dangerous thing we got up to was ice-hopping. Together with our friends we cut the ice into squares, stretching forward in a long line over the pond. The aim was to run across these squares, hopping from one to the other, the winner being the one who got to the far side of the pond without mishap.

On one attempt (our last), Jock landed too far off the centre of one of the ice-squares. It tipped up, plunging him into the icy water. The ice-flow then settled back into place, leaving him trapped underneath. Thank God he didn't slip under the solid ice around him. We frantically pulled the ice-flow out of the way and I managed to reach down and grab hold of his arm. We dragged him out, frozen, wet, and shaken, but not stirred.

Unfortunately, as he would have died of hypothermia otherwise, we had to get him straight home to change and warm up. This meant that we had to come up with a logical explanation for him being wet through. The truth would have earned us a beating for our stupidity.

Harold did his best. "A Golden Eagle flew past and pished on him," he explained.

Dad looked sceptical.

"It might have been James," I ventured.

He still didn't look convinced.

Little Harold decided on a less subtle approach. "He

was running across the ice and he fell in the pond," he piped up before we could stop him. Our frosty glares froze him as solid as Jock's ice-bound eyebrows, but it was too late. We were in big trouble.

Harold was the first to recover. "It was him, not us," he blurted out, pointing an accusing, but not totally truthful, finger at Jock.

Dad got out his cane, and Jock was thawed out quicker than an ice-cube in an Afghan's underpants on a summer's day. Our ice-hopping escapades came to an abrupt end.

At school, I was still an underachiever. I was not interested in lessons, and a vestigial desire to perform badly, and thereby get to sit closer to the lovely Miss Munn, still influenced my attitude, even though I knew she was two hundred miles away in Belfast and my new school did not have a seating system based on merit (or lack thereof).

I was also having difficulty with my handwriting. My teachers described it as 'illegible'. I proudly announced this to my parents, but they insisted it wasn't a good thing.

In hindsight, I now realise that it was my teachers who had difficulty with my handwriting, and not me at all. I could read it perfectly well, and still can. In fact I'm the only world expert on my handwriting, and I take pride in that. It does mean, however, that this book that you're reading bears little resemblance to the handwritten manuscript that I sent to the unfortunate typist. The original was much better of course. It's also been published forty years after I wrote it, as it took her that long to decipher it.

In Limavady, I had been taught to write with single, defined letters. In Belfast, they taught me joined-up writing, where every single letter was joined to the next. In Scone, we were told to join only certain letters. Letters that did not flow easily into the next were to be left unjoined. The way we were taught to write letters differed between my various schools, so I'd write any particular letter in several different ways, depending on how the muse took me at the time. For example, I'd sometimes write 's' instead of 's', 'f' instead of 'f', or even, on occasion, I'd write 'p' instead of 'p'. Now they may all look the same to you but if you'd seen my original, handwritten manuscript, then you'd know what I'm talking about – at least you would if you could read it.

This caused me some confusion and, if the writer is confused, it is pretty certain that the reader will be. My teachers were not impressed and gave me a hard time.

Teaching is the only job where the bad workman blames the end product for their own shoddy workmanship. How many artists do you hear complaining that the only reason they haven't achieved fame and fortune is because their paintings are crap? *'I'd have been successful if I'd painted the Mona Lisa,'* they'd moan. *'How am I meant to get to the top with the rubbish that I've created? It's not fair! Leonardo had it easy!'* And yet teachers do it all the time. *'John's handwriting is appalling,'* they'd put in my school report. *'His arithmetic is pathetic, and his spelling beggars belief.'* Not once did they mention that it was them who'd taught me those things!

This half-printed, half-joined-up writing that we were

taught, led to us writing slower than our fully joined-up contemporaries. In my case this was magnified by my confusion at being taught in various different styles, and by the natural slow speed with which I approach life in general.

'*John is either lazy or stupid,*' my teacher wrote in my report, '*and, as I don't think that he's stupid, then he must be lazy.*'

She never wrote, '*John is laid-back and relaxed, and takes life at a pace that will ensure he is never stressed. No doubt he will grow up happy and healthy, unlike my crabby, bitter and high blood-pressured self.*'

The slowness of my writing did, however, cause me problems at university, as I couldn't keep up with the lecturers. I spent most evenings copying up other students' notes, and my social life suffered. I realised that I had to do something about this so I reversed the process, spent most evenings going out, and my work suffered. Consequently, I was thrown out at the end of my first year – but that's another story.

At this early stage of my academic career, no one would have envisaged me going on to Further Education, my school record was so poor. I was now in Primary Seven, and about six months away from the dreaded Eleven Plus exams. Halfway through the term, my teacher walked down the aisle during a history lesson and caught me unawares. She spotted the meaningless scribbles and doodles that I had been scrawling over the pages of my exercise book while pretending to take notes. This was a favourite ploy of mine. If the teacher approached, I'd turn to a fresh page and start writing properly. But on this occasion, I was too slow and she caught me. I tried to tell her that it was just my poor handwriting, but she was having none of it. She promised me there and then that she was going to get me through my Eleven Plus, whether I wanted to pass it or not, and she worked me hard from then on, keeping a beady eye on me every lesson.

This was a big turning point for me, and I owe a big thank you to Miss X, Class of 1969, Robert Douglas Memorial School. I thrived on the extra attention I was given and began listening in class. I even thumped Titchy Taylor for snapping my pencil in half. A few weeks earlier I would have thanked him and broken his as well, so that neither of us would have had to do any writing.

Determined to avenge my badly savaged pencil, I waited for Titchy Taylor after school. Now, as you've probably guessed from his name, Titchy was not the biggest lad in class, but he did have a fearsome reputation as a fighter, aided by the fact he had a lot of big, nasty friends in the Secondary School we were combined with. I was therefore a bit nervous as I waited for him by the school wall. But fate was on my side. Either oblivious to the possibility that I would be annoyed with him for breaking my pencil, or full of cockiness because of his reputation and his connections, he climbed up the steep bank directly in front of me, then started to scramble over the wall. As he reached the top, his head was at the perfect height and I hit it with all my might. He disappeared back over the wall and somersaulted down the bank, landing in a whimpering heap at the bottom.

As he made no attempt to get up, I brushed my hands together then sauntered nonchalantly into the park opposite. But two of Titchy's mates caught up with me. They'd seen my meticulously executed ambush and misinterpreted it as a sneak attack. They were of the opinion that I should wait where I was until Titchy arrived to beat me up. I reluctantly agreed to their proposition.

Titchy duly arrived in a loud and agitated state, and espoused the same strange opinion as to the nature of my attack. I therefore invited him to do his worst, face-to-face. He quickly became less enthusiastic about what he was going to do to me, and slunk off muttering that he'd get his big mates to rip me apart. This was an honour in itself but not one I was looking forward to (a bit like being asked to make love to the Queen Consort). However, the threats came to nothing and all my limbs remained attached.

It was also easier to concentrate now because my class had moved away from the main school due to overcrowding. We were relocated to 'The Institute', a few hundred yards from the main school. It was quiet and easier to study with fewer distractions around. Dad didn't like it when I told his friends I had been taken out of school and put in an institution, but the more he tried to explain, the more they would smile their sympathy and nod their heads in condolence rather than agreement.

I was ill during the Eleven Plus exams and had to sit them on my own the following week. This suited me. There were no distractions and I passed, though not with flying colours.

In Scotland at the time, there was a three-tier school

system. This consisted of the Academy, which was the Grammar School; the Secondary Modern, for the no-hopers; and the High School, which was somewhere in between, poaching the thickest of the Academy-bound, and the cleverest of the Secondary Modern-bound children as its pupils.

I was down for the Academy, as I'd passed my Eleven Plus, but was desperate not to go. Its pupils were regarded as sissies, and they used to be attacked by gangs of yobs (including me) as they made their way home from school.

This particular year, the Academy was over-subscribed and so colluded with the High School to persuade the parents of border-line children like myself, to send them to the High School instead. They told my parents that I would respond better to being near the top of the class at the High School, rather than the bottom at the Academy. (Knowing me, they were probably right). Mum was sympathetic to my heart-felt pleas, but Dad was set on me going to the Academy. Luckily Mum's nagging persuaded him to at least have a look at the High School. When he found out they played rugby rather than 'soccer', as he called it, he changed his mind, declared that it was a good school, and I won the day.

To say I was relieved would be an understatement. The thought of having to get off the school bus, rip off my Academy blazer, then join my old friends before beating up my new schoolmates, had not appealed to me at all.

Jock not only stayed on at the Secondary Modern, but was actually held back for a year as he could not (would not) keep up with the meagre standard required. This was less a reflection on his academic ability than on the energy with which he was pursued by Big Morag and a bevy of other older girls who had taken a shine to the overgrown big lummox since he had moved to the secondary school. He was in great demand. It was a new experience for him and he didn't know if he was enjoying it or not. He spent half the time looking happy, and the other half looking terrified.

I had also come to the notice of the fair sex. The Brownies annual dance was fast approaching, and Leslie asked me to be her escort. Her rash of freckles and moon face reminded me of my first love, Sylvia, but I was too much of a gentleman to refuse, so I agreed to turn up on the night.

The big day soon arrived and, dutifully, so did I. Each dance, I arose and did the gentlemanly thing, dancing with the rather plain girl who'd invited me. All the time though, I had my eye on Jane, the girl I fancied. Everyone fancied her as a matter of fact. She was the belle of the school. She had had her pick of the lads and, typical of a woman, she picked a strapping great big one, when she could have had me! Cameron was his name, and probably still is.

As the last dance was announced, love blinded me to manners, my sense of duty, and my sense of self-preservation. Forgetting all about Leslie, I marched over and asked the object of my dreams to dance. Taken by surprise, she agreed, and I whipped her onto the dance floor for a smooch before her large and somewhat bemused date could gather his wits and object. He quickly recovered though and, not wanting to be left sitting on his own looking like Billy-no-mates, he rapidly secured a dance with the second most sought after young lady at the do. The next few minutes were total chaos as this process was frantically passed on down the pecking order until the Brownies' carefully laid plans were totally upset. Everyone was having the last dance with someone other than the person they'd arrived with.

I say 'everyone', but that's not quite true. The lights were turned down low for this last, romantic song. When they came back up again, I noticed Leslie, sitting on her own, crying. I had total forgotten about her in my moment of triumph with the school beauty, and I felt a right bounder. Before I could feel the left bounder, Big Cameron spotted me and came bounding after me with vengeance burning in his vengeful visage. I fled the scene leaving Leslie, Jane, Big Cameron, and my dignity far behind. But I still had a big grin on my face next morning.

I later tried to avoid a similar situation when, at Perth High School, a young lady asked me to take her to the First Year Disco. I politely refused, telling her that I was not going to the dance. I knew the mayhem that agreeing to a date could cause. When I duly arrived on my own, she didn't look too happy. There's no pleasing women, is there? She was standing with my old friend Liz, and a tall, gangly girl who was well over six feet in height.

Being a dedicated Scottish Country dancer, I did not care for the newfangled disco dancing but, when the DJ put on *The Gay Gordon's*, I felt that I should do the decent thing and dance with the girl who had invited me. As I approached, she turned to Liz and said loudly and condescendingly, "Here he comes!"

Not appreciating being taken for granted, and not being one to turn the other cheek, I marched straight past her, nose in the air, and asked the giant stick insect to dance. Liz and her friend screamed, whether in horror or delight, I don't know.

I soon began to regret my impetuous reaction. *The Gay Gordon's* is not designed to be danced with a girl who is three feet taller than yourself. I could not even attempt to get my arm around her shoulders, but we managed to improvise, and crabbed our way painfully around the dance floor. It was when she attempted to spin under my arm that we fell into real difficulties. She went through all sorts of contortions during the attempt – bent double, a hernia threatening.

Out of the corner of my eye, I could see Liz and my should-have-been partner. Instead of looking suitably chastised by my impromptu action, they were rolling about the floor in hysterics. This wasn't the reaction I'd been after. This was embarrassing enough, but the hysteria began to spread amongst the dedicated disco dancers who were sitting out the Scottish Country Dances. As the merriment grew, it started to infiltrate the ranks of our fellow *Gay Gordoners* who, two by two, dropped out to watch, holding their sides and gasping for breath as they rocked with laughter. Before long we had the whole dance floor to ourselves, while a large and appreciative audience looked on through tear-filled eyes.

My face set in a stubborn frown, I determined to finish the dance. My partner was not made of such stern stuff and her struggles to leave the dance floor while I hung doggedly on to her, further added to the delight of the spectators.

After what seemed like an eternity (I'm convinced the bugger on the DJ stand kept repeating it deliberately) the music finally ended, and we slunk off to loud, enthusiastic, mocking applause.

Later in the evening some of the lads asked if I'd like to join them outside for a fight against the kids from the Catholic school next door. They'd seen me wrestling with the tall girl on the dance floor, and they thought I'd make a useful addition to their gang. Apparently, it was a quaint tradition that they'd turn up at each other's school dances, and do battle in the playground. I refused as I was in a bad mood and was determined not to enjoy myself.

This 'Catholic versus Protestant' thing surprised me. I had only been vaguely aware of it in Ulster, and hadn't realised it was a thing in Scotland as well. It was not until I started secondary school that I noticed it. On the school bus that took me from Scone to Perth for my first day at my new school, everyone was singing, 'The Sash' and other 'Orange' songs. At first I thought they were taking the micky out of me because I was from Belfast. It only slowly dawned that it had nothing to do with me.

My first day at Perth High School could have been a lot worse. Dad was determined to send me to school in short trousers because he had only splashed out on them the year before, and thought they had a couple of years wear in them yet. He was too mean to buy me a pair of long trousers for secondary school. However, my total despair, combined with Mum's pleas on my behalf, finally got through to him and he relented. When I arrived at the school there was not one pair of short trousers in sight. I would never have lived it down if I'd arrived in mine. I might not even have lived. The school was tough enough without appearing on your first day wearing a neon sign saying, 'I'm a prat. Beat me up Scotty.'

School tradition had it, as school tradition always does, that first years were initiated by having their hapless heads shoved down the toilet, which was then flushed. This apparently happened even if you were wearing long trousers. This age-old myth, used all over the country to scare youngsters moving up to 'big' school, was taken at face value at this establishment and there were a few flushed-looking first years at the end of lunch break. For the first time in my life I was glad that Dad drenched my hair with oil every morning. The bullies thought I'd already had my head down the toilet, and they left me alone. The rest of the time I cursed him and my enforced hairstyle. Despite the copious amounts of oil on my head, my hair was still not used to being swept back, and it wouldn't behave itself. As a result, a wad of greased-up hair hung down over one eye while the rest was plastered back to my skull. I soon acquired the nickname, 'Hitler'.

I pleaded with me parents to let me change my hairstyle as it was the late sixties and most kids had long hair while Jock and I were still short back and sides, Brylcreem boys. (Harold and Little Harold escaped the treatment as Dad thought you shouldn't start 'training' your hair until you

171

were heading for secondary school). Eventually they gave some ground to my pleas, and said that I didn't have to grease my hair but I had to keep it short. I tried changing my hairstyle but, every time I did, Mum and Dad teased me, saying I looked terrible. Eventually I agreed to go back under the grease. It was easier to put up with teasing at school than at home.

Peter lent me a pair of boots for the rugby team trials. It was decent of him because we'd had a fight the day before, but young lads tend not to carry grudges after a dust up. None of us had played rugby before, so nobody knew what they were doing. It was a bit like playing for the Scottish national side.

We entered the gym to sign up for the trials, and found the various team positions on notices pinned around the walls. You had to stand under the position in which you wanted to play, then a teacher came around and took your names. I only knew 'scrum-half', as that's where Dad said I should play as I was the right build for it. The problem was that half the school were lined up under that sign. I was determined to be picked for the team and so headed along the gym until I found the shortest queue. Luckily, in view of my size, this turned out to be right wing and not prop forward.

The choice proved to be a good one. Not only were there fewer rivals in the category but, being on the wing, I was close to the selectors on the touchline. They shouted out and coached me as we played, telling where to stand, what I should be doing, and where and when I should be doing it. When the ball eventually came to me (it can take a long time for the ball to reach the wing in schoolboy matches) I hung grimly onto it and set off through the enemy lines. No-one was going to get the ball off me – not by a tackle, and definitely not from a pass. I'd finally got it and I was determined to keep it, no matter what. I weaved my way through the defence and was nearing the try-line when I was kicked up in the air by Duncan, a big lad whose voice had already broken. My voice broke after the tackle, going up several octaves, instead of down. This foul deprived me of my big moment of scoring a try, but I had been noticed, and I made the team.

I was very pleased that everything had gone to plan, despite Dad's insistence that I should have tried out for scrum-half. It was not until our first match that I realised my mistake. Scottish winters are very cold, and so are Scottish wingers, especially at schoolboy level. They rarely touch the ball as someone invariably drops it before it carries as far as the wing. Either that or the statutory, greedy schoolboy centre refuses to pass it. On the odd occasion, usually deep into the second half when the centre is tiring and under pressure, he will fling out a pathetic, panic-stricken attempt at a pass in the general direction of the wing. The winger, with his hands and nuts frozen as solid as an Eskimo's earwax from standing around all match with nothing to do, is then supposed to flex his frozen digits, catch the ankle-high pass, and set off at high speed on a jinking, tendon-tugging run to the opposition's try line.

I could jink with the best of them, and my teammates

would often watch in amazement as I carved my way through our opponents' lines. The trouble was I rarely had the ball with me as my hands were too cold to catch it.

On the subject of freezing, Perth High School was housed in a building that should have been demolished before World War I, and was slowly, but surely, demolishing itself. It was falling down around us, with large cracks in the walls allowing blizzards to blow through. The heating system was antiquated and totally inadequate, and the classrooms were extremely cold. In winter we never removed our coats during lessons. The school removed to a brand new, super-duper, purpose-built building – the year after I left, of course.

Dad's itchy feet were playing him up again, and he went to an interview on the south coast of England, for a flying instructor at the Collage of Air Training, at Hamble, Hampshire. He took the job, and put the deposit down on a house he'd seen, all without consulting Mum, which didn't go down too well.

In order to reduce the quantity of goods (our toys, not Dad's gear) that would need to be transported to our new home, Dad held a 'bring and buy sale'. The trouble with bring and buy sales is that people bring stuff as well as buying it, so we found ourselves with more junk than we'd set out with. The demand for our toys and books though, was so good that I had to go into the house and dig out Harold's favourite book, 'Old Yeller'. He'd been hiding it away, but I found it and surreptitiously sold it for thruppence. He found out and never forgave me. We gave the profits of the sale to our local Boys' Brigade. We hadn't planned to, but it seemed only right as the Brigadier, in trying to support us, had bought most of our junk himself.

Harold was very put out at having to move home. He had just won the heart of the delectable Helen, the prettiest girl in Primary Seven. He broke the devastating news to her during lunch. She took the harrowing announcement in her stride and was seeing someone else before Harold had finished his plum duff. Harold moped about for minutes on end, but finally got over it.

Jock, on the other hand, was happy to move. He couldn't cope with the sheer volume of 'Big Morags' who were after his body. He didn't realise at the time that, with the added attraction of a 'foreign' accent (mild Scottish with a residue of Northern Irish, and the odd German twang) he would be in even greater demand amongst the girls in England.

I said that I didn't want to move, because I was being stubborn but, in truth, I didn't really care either way. I was so used to moving that it just seemed to be the natural thing to do.

Little Harold didn't mind moving as he had fallen out with his erstwhile favourite neighbour. She was a fine, old gentlewoman with short, fat, bowed legs. Her home proudly boasted a beautiful, mini-grand piano with curved, hand-carved Queen Anne legs.

"I like your piano's legs, Mrs Cadogan," Little Harold chirped up when Mum took him along to a coffee morning

"Did you hear that?" Mrs Cadogan crowed to the

assembled women. "Did you hear that?" She was pleased that attention had been drawn to her prize asset, and basked in the reflected glory. "That child has taste!" She turned to Little Harold, prolonging the moment. "What is it that you like about them, child?"

"They look just like yours," he concluded loudly, as coffee sprayed out from several pairs of closely compressed lips as their owners struggled with the choice of laughing or choking.

Mrs Cadogan was mortified.

Young Bon didn't know we were moving until we arrived in England. "Ushbon," she said, and she may well have been right.

CHAPTER 8

PEACE

The journey down from Scotland was a long one. Dad had squeezed us children into the overloaded car as an afterthought, and it was an extremely uncomfortable five-hundred-mile journey. He did make the concession of an overnight stop. This was at a guest house two miles away from our new home, though we didn't know that at the time. We thought we were still miles away. Having loaded up and piled into the car again the following day, we were rather surprised when we arrived at our destination five minutes later and had to unload again.

The house came as an unpleasant surprise as well. Dad had told us all about it in vivid, if totally fabricated, detail, and we were all eagerly looking forward to seeing this mansion we were moving to. This had been his sales pitch to lessen our objections to being uprooted yet again and moved to England. It was also to sweeten Mum as, once again, he had bought a house without telling her and without her seeing it.

The house was called, 'Hillside', which conjured up

images of a beautiful location on a hill, with views all around. Dad had told us that it was situated at the end of a three-mile-long lane, which gave the impression that it would be standing in splendid isolation with countryside all around, and no nasty neighbours to nick our footballs when we accidentally kicked them through their greenhouses. He said that the house had five bedrooms, three bathrooms, a kitchen, a dining room, a sitting room, a games room, a hairdressing salon, and a room with a beautiful redbrick fireplace.

In reality, the house was situated by a bump in the road on a busy, built-up highway. It had three bedrooms. The fourth 'bedroom' was in fact a corridor leading to the third bedroom. The fifth 'bedroom' was the attic, that he never got round to converting. The hairdressing salon was the sitting room to be, after we had ripped out all the washbasins (the house had previously been a hairdressers, but they couldn't sell it as a going concern). The games room and the room with the redbrick fireplace turned out to be one and the same, so Mum claimed it as the living room, and our games room, the one that had been used to persuade us to come all that way with barely a murmur of protest, disappeared at a stroke. Finally, the three 'bathrooms' turned out to be one bathroom, the hairdressing salon with its washbasins (which we promptly ripped out), and an outside bog.

We were all very disappointed, including Mum who was not in on the scam and had been hoodwinked along with the rest of us. It was a shame really because it was, and is, a pleasant, spacious, detached house, but we had

178

been given such high expectations by Dad's sales pitch, that the reality was a huge let down. Dad always was one for hyperbole – probably because of his long legs.

As I've mentioned, the house had been a hairdressing salon and, while it was being converted back into a residential property, we moved into a prefab belonging to the flying school that Dad was working for. At the far end of this lane was the local scout hut which stood on land owned by the flying school. The lease was up for renewal and, at the same time, a new principal had just been appointed at the flying school. The scoutmaster, who had not yet met the new principal, was probably somewhat nervous about the situation. Now, as it happens, the big house at the end of the lane was the official residence of the principals of the flying school. We moved into the small prefab next door but, for some reason, our humble abode was number one, with the principal's house having a name only. When Dad turned up at the scout hut he was informed that there was a long waiting list to join. He put our names on the list and gave our address as, 1 Hamble House Gardens. This had a galvanising effect on the scoutmaster, and my brothers and I mysteriously jumped the queue and were accepted into the Sea Scouts before the ink on the address on the application form had dried.

I am sure Dad would not have deliberately misled them into believing that he was someone other than who he was but, on the other hand, neither would he have disillusioned them if they had jumped to the wrong conclusion after, perhaps, the faintest of nudges in that direction.

Despite Dad's fine efforts to get us in in the first place,

179

Jock soon decided that the seafaring life, the ging-gang-goolying, and the dib-dib-dobbing, were not for him, and he left the Sea Scouts. He felt that it compromised his cool image, and he wanted to concentrate on chasing women. Ironically, he ended up ging-gang-goolying, and dib-dib-dobbing at a far greater rate than the rest of us, but he had considerably more fun doing it. It's funny how life goes round in circles, isn't it? There's no point in running away from anything as, the faster you run, the sooner you catch up with it.

With Jock putting the Sea Scouts behind him, and Little Harold putting them in front of him (he was too young to join) it was left to Harold and I to carry the flag. We carried a big red one because Ted Heath's yacht, 'Morning Cloud', was moored in the village marina. Along with our fellow Sea Scouts, we canoed along behind him at every opportunity, shouting, "Vote Labour!" Very childish perhaps, but then we were children, and children often are. I even managed to board her once (Morning Cloud, not Ted Heath). The yacht was moored at the marina and there was no one on board so I jumped on and off again, just so I could say that I had. That's another reason for keeping this autobiography anonymous – I don't want to be charged with trespass or piracy although, as I only managed to get one leg on the deck before retreating, I might only be charged half-board. It doesn't say much for the security measures taken to protect the Prime Minister though.

Another famous character that I came into contact with, was the round-the-world yachtsman, Sir Robin Knox-Johnston. Unfortunately for me, several months after setting off on an attempt to circumnavigate the globe single-handed, he came back again. I had recently finished school, and was filling in the time before starting sixth-form college, by working the summer holidays at one of the local yacht marinas. I was an odd-job man, fetching and carrying, emptying bins, changing toilet rolls, and generally catering to the berth-holders' every whim. I was, in fact, one of the infamous, 'Berty's Boys', Berty being a well-known local character and harbour master.

One day fate found me alone, holding the fort in the Harbour Master's office, when the phone rang. I ignored it for as long as I could, but the caller was very persistent and the annoying noise eventually persuaded me to pick up the receiver.

"About time," a posh voice barked at me. "Anyhow, just phoned to let you know thet one intends to come up rivaa, rope the old boat what, between two pontoons in ordaa to test the jolly engine."

This would have blocked the entrance to part of the marina, preventing anyone from sailing in or out.

"Well, actually," I plucked up the courage to reply, "we're rather busy at the moment. Perhaps if you tried later…?"

"Not too busy for *me*, I take it?" the voice interjected. "One will only be an hour or so."

I found some confidence and said firmly, "I'm afraid we really are too busy at the moment. You can try later in the evening, but I can't promise anything."

"Who is this?"

The voice sounded distinctly irritated. The tone worried

me.

"Well, I...whe... ehm... ummm!" I spluttered confidently.

There was an ominous silence for a moment.

"To whom am I speaking?" the voice insisted, calmly and quietly, but with unpleasant undertones in its easily assured authority.

My bowels rumbled unhappily as I tried to work out my best escape strategy, self-preservation my main concern.

"To WHOM am I SPEAKING?" The voice demanded an answer.

"I'm the cleaner," I blurted out untruthfully.

"**WHAAATT**!!? It was a scream of outrage and disbelief. "I'm Robin Knox-Johnston. I'm the Managing Director of this firm, and I'm NOT going to be told what to do in MY OWN BLOODY COMPANY, by **ANY BLOODY CLEANER**!!!" The voice, already at ear-splitting levels, rose to a crescendo at the end.

I did the honourable thing. I hung up, abandoned my post, and fled to the toilet where I later insisted I had been for the past two hours with a bad case of diarrhoea. Apart from the onset time that I gave, this was not far from the truth. The yacht and its eminent owner, never appeared, but I seem to recall the cleaning firm being mysteriously replaced by the end of the week.

I'd like to take this moment to apologise to Sir Robin. At least you now know who it was – or you would if this autobiography wasn't anonymous.

Winter in the Sea Scouts was boring, but we put up with it because of the summers of boating and camping. The main pastime during the cold months was trying to prise Charles out of the Scout-hut kitchen where he always bolted when we started a game of British Bulldog. Our version of the game consisted mainly of jumping on Charles.

Charles was not his real name. I have changed it to save him from any embarrassment should he still be alive, which is doubtful if he remained in the Scouts for much longer. On one occasion, during summer camp, we were on a clifftop hike near Poole in Dorset. Everyone walked up to the cliff and looked over the edge. Everyone, that is, except for Charles and my good self, who were both afraid of heights. I eventually plucked up the courage to take a look. However, I didn't stand up like the rest of them, but crawled to the edge on my belly, and looked over. My bowels turned to water. The cliff cut in underneath, giving the impression I was lying in mid-air with nothing to support me. Vertigo set in and I felt as though my legs were lifting up behind me and that I would pitch forward over the cliff. I closed my eyes and forced my unwilling limbs into action, inching slowly back from the edge.

Luckily for me, my timidity (or common sense) went unnoticed because the wolf pack had spotted Charles cowering far from the cliff edge. They scented fear. Fear and sport.

Being boy scouts, they decided it was time to do their good deed for the day, and help Charles get over his fear of heights. Four of them pounced on him, grabbed a limb each, and dragged him, squealing in terror, to the brim of the precipice. Once there, they began to swing him over the edge while the rest of the pack sang, 'If I Had the Wings of a Seagull,' to drown out his petrified screams. As they swung him they chanted, "One, two, three, GOOOO!" On the command, one blathering idiot actually let go of one of his legs, but the rest hung on manfully and managed to prevent him going over the edge. Charles didn't seem to appreciate this kind gesture, and carried on screeching like a Screech Owl with a PhD in screechology.

"Now, now boys," said Skipper Skid, as he sauntered past, earnestly studying an upside-down map. "Less of the skylarking."

With Summer Camp behind us, and the prospect of another long, boring winter stuck inside the Scout hut, Harold and I announced our intention to follow in Jock's footsteps, and leave the Sea Scouts.

"You're not leaving the Scouts," Mum insisted. "Not until you find something else to do."

This was an unexpected turn up. We told Mum about Charles's experience on the cliff top, hoping she would relent, but she was having none of it.

"I'll have less of your lies," she scolded us. "You're not leaving until you find something else to occupy your time."

Harold turned to judo and thereby secured his release from the Sea Scouts. I never did find anything else to do, but Mum finally relented and allowed me to hand in my woggle when I pointed out that I was thirty-three years old and my shorts no longer fitted.

Harold's judo antics rekindled Dad's old enthusiasm for the sport, and he regularly took us all to the gym at his workplace, where he taught us various throws, chokes, strangles and arm locks. I couldn't go to the judo club because classes were on a Saturday and clashed with the hockey matches I played for the school. Nevertheless, with me still being in the Sea Scouts, I got far more practice using the moves that Dad had taught us than Harold did at his judo club.

One day, when there was no hockey match on, I went to watch Harold at the judo club. I thought it was brilliant. I totally fell in love with judo, and couldn't wait to get on the mat and start fighting. Next Monday I plucked up the courage to tell the hockey coach, the fearsome 'Flash', that I didn't want to play for the school anymore as I was going to do judo on Saturday mornings. He flew into a rage, refused to let me hand in my hockey stick, and told me to go away and think very carefully before letting down myself, my teammates, the school, my family, the Queen, and the country as a whole. The following Saturday, while I was still thinking about it, I went along to the judo club with Harold, but this time I had a go. I loved it. All the moves that Dad had taught us in the gym worked, and I found myself throwing fellow 'beginners' in all directions. I was totally hooked.

On the Monday, I returned my school hockey strip to Flash. He took it without speaking, and walked away with a face that would have frozen the snot in an elephant's nostrils. Soon afterwards I was called in to see my House Master. He was a fearsome tyrant affectionately known as, 'Sweaty', and I was one of the some who feared him. He loved our family surname as he could really make it resound as he bellowed it down the school corridors, and he knew there would usually be at least one of us within earshot. My hand shook as I turned the door knob to his office, and I shuffled in after my timid knock had been answered with an ear-splitting screech of, "**ENTER!**"

I was scared but quietly determined to stand my ground, come what may. Sweaty began by asking me about judo. After a nervous start I warmed to the theme, and he must have been caught up by my enthusiasm because we spent most of the time chatting about that. It was only at the very end that he asked, "You won't change your mind then?" I confirmed that I wouldn't, and that was the only reference he made to the school hockey team. I was pleasantly surprised. He was as nice as pie about it. It would have been a different story of course if I had refused to play for the House rather than merely for the school, but I played football and tennis and ran for the House, so was forgiven other non-House related indiscretions.

"Don't worry, I'll sort things out with Flash...I mean Mr M," he assured me as I left his office.

If indeed he did try to plead my case, the pleas fell on deaf ears. Flash did not intend to let the matter drop. At Parents' Evening soon after, he rounded on my father and gave him a lecture on loyalty and what he called, 'old-fashioned values.' Dad stuck up for me and said that looking after your own interests was even more old-fashioned and went back to the amoeba. He was very proud of his riposte and often retold the anecdote, though why he thought that comparing me to an amoeba would impress people, I will never know.

Flash was to have one last run-in with my family before he decided it might be safest to bury the hockey stick. During a P.E. lesson, and still simmering after his unproductive encounter with my father, he found himself refereeing a hockey match in which my brother Harold was playing. Harold was well aware of the ongoing 'Hockeygate' feud and, when certain decisions didn't go his way, he suspected the reason why, and was becoming a little agitated. Now Harold has never been one to allow a family feud to carry on without him making his own small contribution and so, when a decision was eventually given in his team's favour, he brushed the other hopefuls aside and stepped up to take the free hit, himself.

Never one to turn the other cheek, and with pent-up frustration bubbling inside him, Harold stepped up to the ball. He raised his hockey stick high above his head, his body coiled like a spring. His mighty, but premature, swing, sent the ball rocketing towards Flash, who had his back to it, whistle in mouth, preparing to blow for the free hit to be taken.

"DUCK," some toady yelled.

He ducked.

This was a mistake.

As he bent over, the ball caught him square in the ring-piece at a hundred miles an hour, and wedged solid between his bum-cheeks. He blew his whistle so hard that the pea shot out.

My decision not to play hockey again was finally accepted the following morning.

But I'm running away with myself again. We had yet to start school in England, and were sitting watching the goldfish bowl as Dad still refused to buy a television. He eventually relented and, after five years deprivation, we finally had a telly again, albeit a black and white one with a nine-inch screen. We were fascinated by this strange 'new' technology and, each evening we all sat glued to the goggle box – all, that is, except for Harold, who preferred to stick with the goldfish bowl.

Harold had always been interested in wildlife, and still is – though it is now a different kind of wild life that interests him. He was once made an honorary member of the Scottish Society for the Prevention of Cruelty to Animals (SSPCA) when he discovered two abandoned owlets during one of his treks through the woods. Their nest had been blown out of a tree and mummy owl had given up on them and flown away. Harold named them Cuthbert and Clarence, contacted the SSPCA, then led them back to the owlets. I accompanied them and thereby also obtained an honorary membership, much to Harold's chagrin as I had done nothing to deserve it. It may surprise you that Harold managed to find his way back to the owlets at all, but his woodsmanship and sense of direction had improved dramatically since his first foray downstream to become lost in the forest. In fact he had been lost so often that there was now nowhere within a ten mile radius of our house that he had not been lost in, so he knew the area better than any living soul.

My sense of direction has always been good. Good, at least, in two dimensions. My vertical sense of direction sometimes lets me down. Once when I was five, we were staying at a hotel for the weekend. Having finished dinner we climbed the stairs to retire for the night. I ran on ahead but, when the rest of the family reached our hotel room, I was nowhere to be seen. They searched high and low but, unfortunately, not high enough. There was no sign of me, and eventually Mum and Dad called in the management to help. They joined in the increasingly frantic search. Still no sign. Then Mum spotted that the stairway to the next floor had been cordoned off, as those rooms were being refurbished. "He'll be up there," she said.

The manager didn't believe for one minute that I'd have been stupid enough to have crawled through the barriers, and was waiting patiently upstairs for the rest of my family. Mum had to explain to him that I definitely was that stupid. They found me in the room directly above ours, sitting on an unmade bed, arms folded and very indignant. "Where have you been?" I snapped angrily as my relieved family burst in. "I've been here for hours!"

But back to England, and the sleepy little south coast village where we'd recently moved to from Scotland. The prefab we were living in was a remarkable dwelling. Although small on the outside, it was very roomy on the inside – a regular TARDIS. The seven of us fitted in with no difficulty – even Jock who was now fourteen and about seven feet tall. We became quite attached to it (the prefab, not Jock) and were upset when it was demolished in the name of progress – especially as we were still in it at the time.

After an idyllic beginning to life in England, the sad day

came all too soon, when we had to start at our new schools. Harold and Little Harold went to the junior school while Jock and I were at the secondary so, although we'd been split up, at least none of us had to face a new school alone.

In my first lesson I sat next to a boy called John Russel. He emigrated to Australia. This didn't help to make me feel welcome.

The dreaded first lunch break arrived. Jock and I joined forces, our backs to the playground fence, waiting for the inevitable trouble to start, ready to hit the first person to look at us sideways, as instructed by Dad. Half an hour later we were still waiting. Jock looked at me, I looked at him, and we returned to our respective classrooms with puzzled expressions on our puzzled faces. No-one had even bothered to talk to us, never mind attack us! It was all very confusing.

That night we swapped stories with our puzzled-looking brothers. At least some boys had thrown stones at them, but the rest of the school hadn't joined in! Also, the culprits had run away as soon as Harold and Little Harold had retaliated. (Getting into a stone-throwing fight with Belfast boys is not a good idea. The desultory shower of pebbles that had come their way had been met with a fusillade of half-bricks.)

It was all very odd. At first we thought it was some sort of trick to get us to lower our guard but, as the days went by, we came to realise that no-one was particularly interested in attacking us. We slowly settled in to this new way of life. It wasn't as if they were all nice to each other, but they seemed to have their pecking order all worked out

190

and the lower orders didn't fight back if pushed around by someone further up the tree. In Scotland, if you'd rolled over and shown your throat in submission, someone would have ripped it out.

No doubt they had done all their fighting at an earlier age, and were content with their places on the ladder. We were a bit of an anomaly because, as newcomers, we didn't fit into their pecking order, and no-one was keen on risking their place by taking us on. For my part, I was happy not to rock the boat. I was quite enjoying my rest.

There were a few non-violent attempts by lads to try to judge where in the social order I should be, but without risking their status or their skin. One of the boys, the year bully, did try it on with me, but he made sure he did it while there was no one else around, so I guessed that he didn't want to risk backing down or losing in front of witnesses. I called his bluff and invited him to throw the first punch. He declined on the grounds that he had a sore wrist, but said he would sort me out when it was better. I just smiled and he stormed off, and he left me alone after that.

Reading that last paragraph has got me thinking. I hope it was a fight he was after!

I had no more trouble for the next three years. Fights were so rare that, when one did break out, the whole school would run to it and crowd round in a circle to watch the action. This usually consisted of two reluctant boys struggling to get out of the circle whilst being goaded on by the rest of the school to hit each other. In Scotland, if someone wasn't fighting then everyone else would stop scrapping and crowd around them, staring in a mixture of puzzlement and disgust.

Little Harold got so desperate at the lack of action that he manufactured all sorts of excuses to try and start a fight. He found a likely victim down by the shores of the Solent, stamping on ants. Little Harold announced that he loved ants and that if the lad killed another one then he was going to get a good old-fashioned British thrashing.

As I've told you, no one was quite sure where our place in the established pecking order should be, so the poor lad didn't know what to do. He was programmed to obey anyone higher than him, and to push around anyone lower. Little Harold didn't fit into the structure so it didn't compute. He was clearly struggling to find an appropriate response and decided on simultaneous defiance and flight. He stamped on another ant, then ran away as fast as his legs could carry him.

He'd made a schoolboy error though, which was fair enough as he *was* a schoolboy. In his haste to flee, he'd forgotten his bike. Little Harold hid in the bushes and staked it out. Half an hour later the lad crept gingerly back, casting nervous glances in all directions and sniffing the wind for any sign or scent of danger. But Little Harold was well hidden, silent and patient. He wasn't drawn into a premature pounce by any of the lad's feints in the direction of the bike while he scanned the bushes for any tell-tale movement. Little Harold remained stock still and waited for him to enter the kill zone. Eventually, satisfied with his precautions, the lad moved in and reached down for his bike.

Little Harold struck.

With a milk-curdling yell, he leapt out of the bush and was on him before the lad could mount up and make good his escape. The promised 'good old-fashioned British thrashing' was duly administered, and they both came away happy – Little Harold, because he had battered someone at long last, and the other lad because he now knew his place in the pecking order relative to Little Harold, and so everything in his world was once again in its right place. Dibble and Little Harold remain good friends to this day.

In fact, several years later, Dibble joined forces with my brother on another of his stake-outs. By this time they were teenagers and the bike had been replaced by a car. Little Harold's car had been broken into on a quiet lane, and the stereo stolen. The police were extremely helpful, giving him a crime number before promptly closing the case. Little Harold appreciated their sterling efforts, but decided that catching the buggers would be a better policy. For nostalgic reasons, to commemorate their first meeting, Little Harold and Dibble decided that a good old-fashioned British thrashing should be administered as well. Therefore, as they crouched in the bushes in the dark lane where the crime had been committed, Little Harold's newly repaired car parked as bait, they were armed with a baseball bat and a tyre iron, and had their faces hidden by balaclavas.

The sun set and the time dragged slowly by, but my brother, as I've mentioned, can be very patient when lying in wait for a victim and, a good few hours into the night he nudged Dibble awake. There, on the far side of the car, they could make out two dark figures acting furtively.

They synchronised their watches.

Sending Dibble round the back of the car to cut off their escape route, Little Harold crept round the front then, at the appointed second, they both leapt out, brandishing their weapons and screaming at the top of their voices. Their screams, loud and blood-curdling though they were, were drowned out by the screams of the poor courting-couple they had trapped between them.

Apologising profusely, and turning down all offers of money and jewellery, the two hooded men shuffled off, slipped into the car and sped away, leaving the thoroughly traumatised lovers far in their wake.

This incident caused Dibble, always a gentle soul by nature, to renounce violence altogether. Alongside the fact that he had not harmed any of God's creatures since Little Harold had given him a beating for stamping on ants, this led him naturally to lean towards Buddha. I had recently bought Mum a small 'future' Buddha – the one with the big belly. She had put it in her garden for ornamental purposes – the thinking woman's garden gnome.

One night I'd been out for a drink with Little Harold and Dibble, and we'd gone back to Mum's house and were having a quiet discussion about religion. Dibble mentioned being drawn to Buddha, so I told him that Mum was a practising Buddhist and that she had a small shrine in the garden. He was very excited and wanted to see it, so I took him outside and pointed to the vague outline in the bushes. It was night-time and he was struggling to see in the dark so I invited him to have a closer look.

Despite the beer, and the fact that he hardly knew me, a little voice of caution in the back of his head made him grow suspicious – after all, I was Little Harold's brother!

"If I bend down to look at it, you're going to kick me up the arse, aren't you?" he said sagely.

I was shocked and assured him that I would do no such thing in front of my mother's shrine to peace and tranquillity.

Satisfied, Dibble bent over for a closer look.

I kicked him up the arse!

This was a lesson in trust that he never forgot, and it has stood him in good stead many times since.

But that day was a still a long way off, and Little Harold was still a young boy, new to the area, and yet to make any friends. A slightly snooty couple lived nearby and did not approve of the local children. They felt that, as Dad was a pilot, then his fourth child might just be acceptable as a playmate for their precious, only son. Little Harold was invited round for a play date. Despite much protest, he was duly dispatched to make a new friend.

When he arrived, Little Harold was allowed up to the lad's bedroom to play (a great honour), while his mother set the table for tea. Three minutes later she heard the drumming of footsteps hurrying down the stairs, a brief, "Goodbye," then the slamming of the front door as Little Harold made good his escape. Hearing sobs, she hurried upstairs and found her beloved boy tied to the radiator. Little Harold wasn't invited back.

To keep him amused and out of trouble, Dad bought

Harold an air rifle!!! We thought this was great, and set up tin cans at the end of the garden, taking turns to fire at them to see who the best shot was. Unfortunately, our neighbour in the house behind was a keen gardener and was out that afternoon, on his hands and knees, weeding around his prize roses. The flimsy hedge at the bottom of our garden didn't prove to be the impenetrable barrier that we had believed it to be, and he ended up having his arse well and truly peppered with lead pellets. For some reason, known only to him, he complained to our parents, and Harold was told to get rid of the gun.

The next day the police arrived. The local bobby was very well informed, and was aware that Harold had recently acquired an air rifle. But his information was slightly out of date and he was informed that Harold had sold it the day before. Apparently, the boy to whom Harold had sold the gun, had had the Brownies pinned down in the Scout hut for an hour as he sniped at them from his vantage point in a nearby tree. Brown Owl had eventually made a break for it under a hail of pellets, and alerted the Flying Squad (PC Smout on his bicycle). Harold had been the initial suspect but, as usual, his alibi was strong, and he was exonerated.

Little Harold had a paper round, and was having problems with a vicious dog at one of the houses he delivered to. He had a similar approach to doggy diplomacy as Dad. He decided that direct action was the quickest way to sort out the matter, and armed himself with a large stick. If my memory doesn't fail me, it was actually a sawn-off rudder handle with a hole drilled through the end which he'd fitted with a leather strap to go around his wrist. So, as you can see, it was a purely spur-of-the-moment decision. When Little Harold marched into enemy territory to deliver the paper, proudly waving his new peace-maker over his head, he was disappointed to find the dog wasn't in the garden. But the owner spotted him, armed to the teeth, and demanded to know what the stick was for.

"It's to beat your dog with," Little Harold explained patiently. Obviously, the man was a bit slow on the uptake. The furious man complained to the paper shop, but the dog was kept indoors from then on when Little Harold made his rounds. The paper shop owner had a quiet word with Little Harold who quoted President Roosevelt: 'Speak softly and carry a big stick'. His boss said that he didn't mind him speaking softly but explained that, unlike Northern Ireland, the English prided themselves on having an unarmed paperboy force.

Meanwhile, back at school, we found the teachers in England were a little more civilized than their Scottish or Irish counterparts. Corporal punishment was dished out as a last, rather than first, second and third, resort. This leniency on their part did not appear to have any adverse effect on the pupils – they were just as unruly as in any other school.

My favourite lesson was physics. This had nothing to do with any love of science, and everything to do with the physics teacher being severely long-sighted. In his lessons the bad lads sat at the front instead of their usual position at the back for other lessons. Tucked up nice and close to the teacher's desk, where they couldn't be seen, they'd bring bread into class and toast it over the Bunsen burners. The teacher's nose would twitch and he'd strain his eyes trying to see what was going on, but the only pupils within the range of his pupils, would be sitting quietly and behaving.

Another pastime for the more adventurous, was to sit at the back in the science lab, and wait until he turned his back to write on the blackboard. The challenge was to climb onto the benchtop at the back and then run, leaping from one bench to the next, to the front, where you had to be seated before he made his long, slow turn to see what the noise was. Our record was transferring the whole backrow of eight boys to the front bench over the course of a lesson. Personally, I got so good at this that I was awarded the school science prize at the end of the year.

The nerve-tingling excitement of these intermittent bouts of naughtiness will be lost on the modern child who carries on in this manner in the full view and knowledge of his or her teacher. The quieter pupil will be forced by overzealous teachers into leaping from desk to desk if they are showing a rebellious and disruptive streak of studiousness. This permissiveness, of course, takes all the fun out of being naughty, and so your average pupil is probably better behaved nowadays than they were back in my day.

Jock's class, the worst behaved in the school, took things even further. The Physics teacher once had them doing a gravity experiment. Two boys were holding two different weights out of the upstairs lab's windows. In their other hands they were holding stopwatches to time the descent.

"On my command," said the physics teacher, "let go…NOW!!!"

Needless to say, two stopwatches fell to their deaths. The two boys remained at the windows with two weights in their hands and innocent, 'you never said which' looks on their faces.

Jock's favourite trick was based on the fact that coal gas (as used by Bunsen Burners at that time) became explosive when mixed with the correct amount of air – a fact that the physics teacher came to regret imparting to his young protégés. There were a number of Belfast sinks in the science lab and, when not in use, they were covered with close-fitting wooden covers. These covers had finger holes at either end for extraction purposes. As his physics class was straight after dinner, Jock and his fellow budding scientists would go up early and stick a gas hose into one of the holes of each cover and fill up the sinks with coal gas. Then, just before class started, they'd remove the hoses and reattach them to the Bunsen Burners so everything looked normal. But it wasn't normal because they had also ignited the gas in the Belfast sinks. The gas would burn silently and invisibly and would be quietly sucking in air through the holes. About fifteen minutes into the lesson, enough air had been sucked in for the gas/air mixture to go critical, at which point a series of deafening explosions would blast the wooden sink covers six foot in the air, causing fear or hilarity, depending on whether or not you were in on it. Eventually all the sink covers were permanently removed and Jock's friends had to amuse themselves by setting fire to Neil Skinner's trousers instead.

Next to science, music lessons were the highlight of the week. Fritz, the music teacher, caught on that several pupils were deserting his classes by jumping out the windows while he was engrossed in piano recitals. (It was a ground floor room – his piano playing wasn't that bad.) He devised a cunning plan to ensure that no-one escaped future lessons. Standing in the doorway, he counted us as we entered the classroom, planning to count us again on the way out. But we were up to this challenge. As I was counted in at the front of the queue, I went straight to the window, jumped out and ran around to re-join the back of the queue. Several others followed my example and Fritz ended up having sixty pupils in a class of thirty-four. He explained his amazing success to the headmaster, who promptly gave him early retirement.

This did not bother him in particular and he happily worked out his notice. The only thing that did upset him, quite understandably, was pupils tampering with his instrument. Jock's class put a lot of effort into one little project. They threaded metallic milk bottle tops together and tied them to the strings of his piano. The awful racked produced when Fritz began to tinkle on the ivories was even worse than usual.

We went one better. In assembly one morning the headmaster spent ten solid minutes in a tirade against the mindless morons who had tampered with a fire extinguisher, pinching the wall-mounted brackets.

"I'm going to find out where those brackets are," he thundered, "even if I have to keep you here all day."

His announcement was greeted with silence.

"I know who the culprits are," he lied through his teeth. "I'm giving you one last opportunity to own up."

The silence grew deeper.

"Whoever has taken them had better confess and tell me where they are, or there will be real trouble."

The silence was deafening now.

The headmaster was the first to crack. "Alright then," he yelled, "whoever has the brackets had better have them on my desk before the day is out, or they'll wish they'd never been born. I warn you, I intend to find those brackets if it's the last thing I do!"

With an irritated flick of the wrist, he signalled Fritz to commence playing the opening hymn of the assembly.

Fritz flexed his fingers over the grand piano then, with a flourish, brought them firmly down on the keys as we waited with hushed breath.

"CLANG...CLANG...CLANGITY CLANG!"

The tense silence was broken by the most dreadful clatter coming from the piano. There was a delayed reaction as people began to catch on that this cacophony of clangourous clanking was beyond even Fritz's considerable discordant repertoire. The whole school then burst into laughter as the piano lid was raised to reveal the missing brackets lying across the strings. The Head was not amused.

When the sombrely dressed Fritz retired soon after, I

organised a whip-round amongst my classmates and bought him the loudest, gaudiest tie I could find. There was a genuine tear in his eye when we presented him with the leaving present. I was unsure if the watering of his eyes was due to emotion or was brought on by the dazzling brightness of his new tie but, as his bottom lip trembled, I began to suspect the former and felt a little guilty that our present had not been a trifle more tasteful. It made me glad that we had bought him something though, as he was genuinely touched. The following day at assembly (his last) he sat on the back of the gloomy stage with his new tie shining forth like a beacon, illuminating the headmaster's farewell speech and causing a larger than usual number of girls to pretend to faint.

The headmaster was fond of his speeches. There was a table situated at the front of the stage, and he had a habit, as he stood up to deliver his monologues, of pushing the table a few inches along while he kept us waiting for his delivery. One April Fools Day, we climbed under the stage early in the morning, bored a hole up through the planking, and screwed the table leg to the floor.

Later, at assembly, the headmaster stood up to speak. As usual he pushed at the table, but it didn't move. He pushed again. Nothing. He spent five minutes staring in consternation at the table and occasionally trying to shunt it along a little. Totally bemused, he said only a few words to the snickering throng, in between half-hearted attempts to shift the table, before sitting down, deflated, his life-long routine upset and his life in turmoil. He retired soon afterwards, a sad and broken man.

CHAPTER 9

AFTER THE STORM

At least once a year, Dad threw himself into a new hobby and, more often than not, we would all benefit (or suffer) as he would involve us in the shenanigans. Once he bought us all table tennis bats, another time, darts, then tennis racquets, then snooker cues. All manner of accessories would be included. We were kitted out in cricket gear, right down to a miniature jockstrap for Little Harold (I believe it still fits). Dad soon tired of that and we were off fishing, hook, line and sinker. Canoes rapidly followed. All of these short-lived fads were accompanied by private tuition which was provided by Dad, who was a self-proclaimed expert at everything. The excellent sporting facilities at Dad's place of work, helped to make many of these things possible without him going bankrupt (again).

Dad's Fads, as they were affectionately known, came and went with equal rapidity, but it kept life interesting and made choosing Christmas presents for him easy. Whatever the current craze was, then that provided the inspiration for his present. We had to be careful with our timing though. If we bought his present too early, then his hobby would have changed. If we left it too late then he would have already bought every conceivable item relating to the hobby.

During Dad's sailing craze, having bought a small dinghy and not knowing how to make it work, he enrolled himself and me on a training course. We were learning on the River Hamble, Southampton Water, and The Solent. With their fast-flowing currents and double tides, conditions can be quite challenging on these waters. To make matters worse, our training course took place on the same week as The Isle of White Power Boat Race, so we were frequently swamped, buffeted or capsized by the wakes of these fast boats.

When we were eventually allowed out in a dinghy for our first 'solo flight', we somehow managed to negotiate the heavy traffic, to emerge from the River Hamble into Southampton Water, still afloat, and still in the boat which was still the right way up. With a stiff breeze at our backs, we soon reached the main shipping lane that we had been warned to avoid – we just didn't know how to avoid it.

With ships bearing down on us from all directions, Dad stood in the bows, frantically waving and shouting at one-hundred-and-thirty-thousand ton tankers to get out of our way, as our dinghy zigzagged uncontrollably in their path with Yours Truly at the helm.

We knew from our theory lessons that sail has right of way over engines. What we didn't know is that the stopping distance for these huge ships is between two and seven miles depending on speed and tonnage. This, coupled with the fact that the width of the deep-water channel did not allow these supertankers to deviate from their course by more than a few yards, meant that Dad's appeals to them to 'get out of the bloody way', were ignored.

With a curse, Dad finally gave up his pointless task at the prow and scrambled back to relieve me of my duties as helmsman. Once there he tried to wrest the bucking tiller from my grasp, but an extremely close encounter with the large and noisy Isle of White hovercraft had left me frozen to it in terror. When he finally managed to use his superior weight (and an oar) to prise me away from the tiller, he took control.

I say 'control', but it would be more accurate to say that he took hold of the helm, because 'control' would not be the first word to spring to mind of even the least nautically-minded bystander. However, the slightly less frenetic lack of control displayed by Dad, set the alarm bells ringing for our instructor who was watching from the shore. When I'd been at the helm, he'd believed that we were engaged in a foolish but disciplined game of chicken with our larger adversaries on the seaway. In fact, he had been secretly admiring the skill, courage and dexterity with which we were handling the dinghy as we surfed down bow waves, dodged giant propellers, and skipped away at the last second from under the bows of each vessel in turn. He had decided to tear us off a strip for our foolhardiness, but deep down he was proud that, in a few short days, he had made such able, if somewhat over-exuberant, seamen of us. But when I relinquished the helm to my father, it soon became obvious that our daring games of tag were not intentional and that we were in difficulties.

Jumping into another dinghy with a couple of more competent students, the sailing instructor managed to catch up with us despite our high speed and the jinking runs we were making. He sailed close by and shouted for us to 'heave to'. Dad had forgotten how to 'heave to' but, with yet another violent change of direction, I managed. I heaved up over the side.

This did not slow us down but it did make our trail easier to follow as we weaved between the other boats and ships.

The wind grew stronger, both externally and internally, and, as the spray became thicker, the instructor was often left tracking us not by sight but by sound. Our screams could be heard from Southampton to the Isle of White. As we shot past him, first in one direction then the other, he shouted out frantic advice over the sound of our wailing. We caught only brief snatches of each instruction but, after about five passes, we thought we had pieced together the message, "Slow…jibe…about…to…heave!"

We tried our best to comply but it didn't help.

He then made several valiant attempts to come alongside but we always managed to elude him at the last second. Eventually, more by luck by judgement, we did succeed in holding steady for long enough for him to board us. Leaving more trusted students to sail his boat back up the river, the instructor took command of ours. As we crawled laboriously homeward against the rapidly ebbing tide, the setting sun glistened alarmingly off his noisily gnashing teeth.

"Not bad for a first effort?" Dad ventured hopefully.

The reply was unprintable.

Dad did eventually pass the course and took his certificate home proudly. He was now entitled to captain any sailing-vessel provided that it was not over thirteen feet in length. I was sent home with nothing but a pat on the back. As pats go it was pretty firm – I was winded.

After our experience in the dinghy, Dad decided that we needed to top up our swimming skills, and he sent Harold and I on a life-saving course. We were eventually awarded the Bronze Medallion in Life-Saving after an intensive course at Southampton swimming baths. It was a gruelling program and, as well as life-saving and resuscitation techniques, included swimming a length of the baths in pyjamas, and recovering a brick from the bottom of the pool.

Living by the sea, as we did, my first opportunity to put my new-found skills to the test was not long in coming. An acquaintance of mine capsized his dinghy in Southampton water. I went into action immediately, but by the time I had struggled into my pyjamas and found a brick, he had gone. I know that the drama of a good death helps to sell a book but I have to admit that, although he had indeed gone, he later came back again. He had righted the boat, climbed back in and sailed his thirteen-foot-long dinghy to France. The French promptly arrested him and sent him home again – minus his boat. His mum was furious because she had been expecting him back for his tea two days earlier. I can't remember what she had cooked, but it was ruined.

"I got lost Mum," he cried, and was forgiven.

Aren't mothers wonderful?

As well as hobbies, Dad also had many health fads where he was convinced that first one substance, then another, was the elixir of life. His least eccentric fad was putting lecithin on his cornflakes. Fair enough. He then took to eating raw carrots. Nothing odd about that. But if everywhere you go you carry a large bag of them and chew away as if your life depends on it, offering one to any passer-by who glances at your carrot, then you tend to gain something of a reputation as an eccentric.

His piss de resistance (excuse my French) was when he discovered cider vinegar. He read that this was good for you and, never being one to doubt the written word, immediately began drinking it by the gallon. He even carried some around in a hip flask. As a flying instructor, this habit did little to instil confidence in his pupils who, out of the corners of their eyes, would look across for some encouragement and see their pilot taking a crafty slug from his hip flask. One of them eventually complained and Dad had some difficult explaining to do.

Our schooldays were coming to an end. Jock had finally taken earlier advice and dropped out. He had a wonderful time at school and failed his exams in spectacular fashion, though he did achieve an 'O' level in woodwork and, despite a sterling effort on his part, he couldn't quite manage to fail English Language. His friends therefore condemned him as a swot and he was ostracized. This, along with radiation treatment, Dad's egg nog, and some 'laying on of hands' by a faith healer, cured his testicular cancer, to the amazement of the doctors who had given him six months to live.

He fought his battle against the big 'C', with great flamboyance and panache. The doctors had told Mum and Dad that the radiation treatment (which was very crude at the time) would make Jock's hair fall out and that he would be sick and lethargic and spend most of his waking hours asleep. So they bought a bed-settee for the living room, assuming that he would struggle to get upstairs to bed, and wanting somewhere for him to lie in the company of his family during the last few months of his life.

Jock never used the bed-settee. In fact he was horrified when I recently told him what it was there for. He hadn't had a clue.

Although he did not use the bed-settee, neither did he climb the stairs to his bed very often. He was determined that, if he had to go (which he accepted as a remote possibility), then he would go out with a bang. He had no intention of taking it lying down – at least not on his own. He had a whale of a time. When he wasn't chasing women (well actually he was *always* chasing women) he was playing in a band (to attract women), or racing banger cars (to impress women).

It couldn't go on forever of course. He eventually collapsed and Mum and Dad took him to hospital, fearing the worst. They were shaking when the doctor took them aside after examining Jock. The doctor told them that they could find no trace of cancer and that Jock had collapsed from exhaustion brought on by excessive, non-stop bonking.

Some time later, he was concerned about abdominal pain and visited his doctor. A card duly arrived from the local hospital asking him to attend, but not explaining what for. When he arrived no one seemed to know what he was there for, and he couldn't put them straight as he wasn't sure either. Eventually he was asked if he minded being examined by students. Foolishly he agreed.

Having been left in the company of two nervous medical students for half an hour, Jock remained as confused as they were as to why exactly he was there and what was wrong with him. The doctor eventually returned and neither of the students could offer a diagnosis, but one of them tentatively suggested that a bottomoptomy might prove revealing.

Jock had to drop his trousers and lie on a couch, facing the wall, with his knees tucked up to his chest. Being a big lad, he couldn't fit in the space available, so the doctor suggested that he shuffle backwards and flop his bottom over the edge of the couch. This, obligingly, he did.

At this moment the door opened and ten medical students filed in and sat opposite him, nervously eyeing his exposed posterior as it eyed them back with equal trepidation. This would have been upsetting enough for Jock, but a strange and ominous squeaking sound then reached his ears. He glanced round in concern and saw a trolley being wheeled in, chock-a-block with the most hideous instruments of torture assembled since the sad demise of the Spanish Inquisition.

The doctor's voice reached him at about the same time as the trolley.

"When inserting a finger up the anus," (Jock's eyes grew wider – all three of them), "don't just bung it up there, as it can be rather painful."

Jock frantically nodded his agreement.

"First stroke the anus gently."

Jock had the strange sensation of having his sphincter massaged simultaneously by a finger and ten pairs of eyes.

"Next, insert the finger."

Ttthhuppp!

The finger was inserted, waggled around and withdrawn again.

Pppuhhtt!

An instrument of torture was selected from the trolley.

"This might be a little uncomfortable," said the doctor truthfully as he rammed a bicycle pump up my brother's poor, unfortunate rectum.

Just as quickly as it had been inserted, his bum ejected it again.

"You need to relax, sir," chided the doctor as he returned from the far side of the room having retrieved the pump. He advanced on Jock, a steely look of determination on his face.

It was inserted again.

BBAARRRRPPP!

Jock shot it across the room again, scattering the watching students in a manner reminiscent of his early anal escapades as a baby.

"You really must relax," ordered the doctor, his face like thunder.

"YOU TRY RELAXING WITH A BLOODY BICYCLE PUMP UP YOUR ARSE," Jock exploded (from the opposite end this time).

The instrument was at length (considerable length) successfully inserted.

If Jock thought that the worst of his ordeal was over, he was sadly mistaken. The doctor now commenced pumping. Jock's bowels began to fill with air causing a very unpleasant sensation. He complained that, this time, his bum really was going to explode, but the doctor kept pumping determinedly away, and Jock's rectum continued to expand.

Eventually, when inflation had hit post-war Germany levels, his torturer stopped pumping and unscrewed the device, leaving a large transparent bung in place. Jock now found himself lying on his side, his bowels full of air, his rectum splayed wide and pointing towards a queue of eager students who took it in turns to peer studiously up his apprehensive orifice.

The worst was still to come. When the examination was finally over and the prodding, prying and peering had come to a halt, the doctor removed the bung from Jock's bum with a deft flick of his wrist – and the use of a crowbar. He then turned to the students and, ignoring Jock who was still lying on the couch with his bare buttocks facing the class, began to hold forth on the relevant points of the anal examination. As he did so, an extremely loud raspberry echoed around the room and continued to resound, non-stop, for a good, solid five minutes as Jock's abused rectum expelled the unwanted air hitherto pumped into it. The doctor didn't miss a beat and continued to air his opinions as Jock cowered, abandoned, in the corner, forgotten but for the sound of his sphincter vibrating like it had never vibrated before and airing opinions of its own.

The good news was that Jock was physically healthy and his symptoms were, according to the doctor, caused by stress – though how you can spot stress by peering up someone's bum, I'll never know. On second thoughts, if you pump someone's bottom full of air then spend the next half hour taking turns to stare up it, it's a pound to a penny that the patient will be suffering from stress.

"Right then, we'll just give it another fifty pumps...Ah! Is that a look of stress I see on your face, sir?"

Brilliant! Medical diagnosis of the highest order.

Harold also enjoyed his time at school though, like Jock, he neglected his studies. That seems to be the secret to happy school-life. I made the mistake of working! However, Harold's reasons for not working were very different to Jock's. Whereas Jock was a happy-go-lucky teenager, Harold was very intense. Jock's lack of study sprang from the fact that he couldn't be bothered with schoolwork because he was too busy having a good time with his friends. Harold, on the other hand, concentrated very hard on his studies – to make absolutely certain that he was not seen to be working harder than or, God forbid, achieving higher grades than his mates.

He always had to be one of the lads no matter what. For example, he turned down the offer to become a school prefect because he thought it would set him aside from his pals. As it happened, his decision set him apart because, in the cause of reverse psychology, the headmaster made prefects of all the roughest, worst-behaved pupils in Harold's year. This was partly because they would have otherwise beaten up the prefects, but it was also an experiment to see if trust and responsibility would bring out the best in them.

It didn't!

A reign of terror began, not seen in this country since the time of Bloody Mary (the queen not the drink). It only lasted six short, bloody weeks, until the Head went back to the time-honoured tradition of making prefects of the wimps, nerds and swots. This at last restored the schooliverse to harmony and equilibrium, with the tougher pupils doing whatever they wanted, the prefects telling tales on them, then the rough elements beating them up for grassing. Order was restored and peace reigned once more.

Little Harold had always been a little bleeder at school and so, like Jock and Harold before him, enjoyed himself. He had a knack for inducing others to do daft things, so that he could enjoy their dirty deeds without getting into trouble himself. He was the leader of a small gang whose pecking order was denoted by how high up the tree they were. This was an actual tree, not a hypothetical one. (Little Harold was never a great one for semantics. If he can't eat it, punch it, or bonk it, then he doesn't think it's worth wasting time on.) Little Harold, at one end of the leadership spectrum, perched on the highest weight-bearing branch whilst Piers Clout, at the other end, had to squat at the foot of the tree. This appealed more to Little Harold's sense of humour than to his ego.

Our sister, Bon, started from very humble beginnings, as most babies do. She was born yellow. Now the more smart-arsed readers amongst you might point out that there are more yellow babies born than any other colour, but the nearest our Mum had been to an oriental was when we went for a Chinese meal in Northern Ireland and two-year old Little Harold had taken one look at the waiter and shouted, "All out, all out. It's a Chinaman!" Where he got that from, we had no idea. Maybe he'd been watching a Fu Man Chu film. But Mum was mortified.

Bon was born severely jaundiced. A series of blood transfusions restored her to a more natural colour (for an Irish girl born in Scotland) but left her with a blind fear of nurses, doctors, hospitals, aeroplanes, men, women, cows, trees, and just about anything else she saw or heard. As soon as she became mobile, she followed Mum around everywhere at a distance of no more than six inches. Any further than that and she'd scream her head off. This went on for about three years before she increased the distance to one foot.

By the age of six though, she'd become a self-confident young lady who knew how to stick up for herself which, with four big brothers in the house, she had to do. Jock, eleven years her senior, once smacked her for some trivial

215

digression which she decided didn't merit the punishment dealt out. She hid round a corner and bided her time. When Jock eventually passed by, she leapt out and punched him in the gonad. He went down like a sack of potatoes and collapsed, helpless, on the floor. Mum had to run in and save him as Bon moved in for the kill.

She wasn't annoyingly precocious though. Having four big brothers meant that she was kept well in order and had to get used to teasing and a bit of rough-housing. After the incident with Jock however, we made sure we weren't too rough with our housing.

At a young age she learnt about death when we heard that one of our neighbours had a heart attack. His wife went to stay with one of their children and Bon noticed that they weren't around anymore and questioned Mum about this strange disappearance. Mum explained as best she could, saying that he'd gone to heaven etc. A couple of weeks later, Bon was out playing in the garden. A high-pitched scream rent the air and she came running into the house, squealing all the way. When Mum calmed her down she claimed she'd seen a ghost. Mum told her there were no such things as ghosts, but Bon insisted that she'd seen our next-door neighbour in his garden.

Mum was fascinated by this supernatural phenomenon and was regaling her friends at a coffee morning with this strange tale when she noticed that they didn't look suitably surprised or impressed.

"He got out of hospital yesterday," they explained.

For some reason we had just assumed that he was dead when we heard that he'd had a heart attack. Once again,

Mum was mortified.

Dad didn't really know what to do with Bon. She was his youngest child, so he had a natural soft spot for her, and he was also mellowing with age, but he had a big problem with her. She was a girl! He'd never brought one of those up before. He'd always treated his boys like the lower ranks in the forces – to be bawled at and bullied until discipline was installed. But this was a girl – his little girl – and he couldn't bring himself to do that. And he didn't have a plan B.

Of course, being a girl, Bon *did* have a plan B, as well as plans C, D, E and F. She wrapped him around her little finger. She'd have been a holy terror if it hadn't been for her older brothers' determination not to let her get away with anything that they couldn't.

Being a sensitive child however, she did leave Dad some dignity and, instead of openly defying him, she occasionally agreed to obey him, leaving him to feel that he was in charge while she snuck off and did whatever she wanted behind his back. A typical teenage example of this was when she agreed to be home by nine O'clock each evening. This gave Dad a sense of power and security, and gave Bon plenty of time to get showered and ready in peace before sneaking out the bedroom window, shinning down the drainpipe, and going to a nightclub with her friends.

My schooldays were about to come to an end. On our last day, the whole year went to the local pub at lunchtime. The landlord served us without question, despite the fact we were all in school uniform, which might have given a more astute person a clue as to our age. We then went back to the school, but the teachers had formed a cordon and wouldn't let us back in – a disgraceful encouragement of truancy, if you ask me. And so ended my school days.

I had been wondering where to finish this book, but I've decided to finish it here and now, with the end of my schooldays. You might think that it's a bit of an abrupt ending, but my printer's run out of ink and, until this is published, I can't afford a refill.

Oh, well! That's life! (Mine anyhow).